WEBB'S

Easy

Bible Names
Pronunciation Guide

Featuring every proper name in the English Bible
(Including the Apocrypha)

General Editor
Steven K. Webb

steve webb
productions

D1596834

Steve Webb Productions
5225 Canyon Crest Drive
Suite 71-152
Riverside, CA 92507

info@EasyBibleNamesGuide.com

www.SteveWebbProductions.com

www.EasyBibleNamesGuide.com

First Edition published June 2, 2012
First Print Edition published June, 2016

www. EmmASAyiNG. com

For LeeAnn.

Table of Contents

Preface

Who should use this guide? Anyone who desires to pronounce the names of people and places in the Bible with confidence. Do you read passages of the Bible in public? This book is for you. In private devotions, do you skip the difficult names? This book is for you.

This book was originally begun as a pronunciation guide for myself as I was recording the Douay-Rheims Audio Bible. When I was commissioned to do that work, I was surprised to find that there was apparently nothing currently in print specifically for the Douay-Rheims version that could help me to properly pronounce names of people and places.

In order to expedite the narration, I began to compile a list of names and carefully researched pronunciations, and that list became the book that you now hold in your hands.

Somewhere along the way, I decided to include the spellings and pronunciations of all the English translations I could find. As far as I know, every spelling of every name in *every English translation* of the Bible is included in this guide.

Since the the genesis of this guide was for the Douay-Rheims Audio Bible, which is a Catholic Bible, names included in the Apocrypha appear here as well.

Great effort has been made to include every English Bible translation's names and places in this work. If the reader would be so kind as to write to me at info@EasyBibleNamesGuide.com if the reader is aware of omissions, I will include additions in subsequent editions of this guide.

It is important to note that in my research, I became aware of the fact that there are differing opinions on the correct pronunciations of many of the names contained in the Bible. Often there really is no one "correct" way to pronounce a specific name. Languages do morph over time, and pronunciations can change.

This guide includes the ***generally accepted*** pronunciations in the United States in the year 2012.

Forward

"Oh for heaven's sake, let's just skip that part!"

Sound familiar? It's the sound of men and women worldwide trying to pronounce a long list of unfamiliar biblical words.

Quite frankly, all too many times people skip over valuable information for fear of public embarrassment. Or heaven forbid that one should make an effort only to hear from a dear saint, "That's not the way I learned it!" Either way, let's just say it is an awkward task for most people.

Now there is a way to get professional and authoritative assistance with their pronunciation. Why did someone not think of this sooner? It would have saved me many anxious hours of worrying about the public reading of names that have no equal in the English language.

For this reason, among others, I believe the Webb's Easy Bible Names Pronunciation Guide is a timely and relevant resource for public reading and personal use. I can personally attest to the diligence of the author. He painstakingly did the meticulous work of recording the Douay Rheims Audio Bible, which I know was a two year project. Each name has been carefully researched and properly pronounced.

The list of unusual names is quite extensive. The pronunciation key is clear and easily understood. The volume of names listed reveals the "Mount Everest" of work that has been accomplished.

I will have one in my professional library and suggest that it would be a valuable addition to the library of any student of the Bible.

Chaplain, Colonel, Steve O'Brien, USAFR

Acknowledgments

This book would not be possible without the encouragement and support of my best friend, my partner, and my wife. Happily for me, those three roles are filled by one person. Listeners to my podcast, Lifespring!, know her as the Lovely Lady LeeAnn. I am deeply indebted to her for the many good things she has brought into my life by her grace, her beauty and her patience. She is the quintessential Proverbs 31 woman.

My three sons, Matthew, Steven and Timothy have sacrificed time with me while I have worked on this book. They have also served to remind me that each of us is a work in progress. I love each of them and am thankful that they are all serving God.

Del Brixey invited me to visit his church when we were high school chums. I was not yet a Christian, but his boldness in asking me to come along with him to that small church in Rowland Heights, California, brought me to the place where I ultimately surrendered my life to a personal and loving Savior and God, Jesus Christ.

I am deeply sorry that over the years I have forgotten the name of the man who was my pastor in 1976-77 at Mammoth Community Church. It was from him that I learned that God has a job for each person in the local church. I taught my first Bible study at that little church at the foot of Mammoth Mountain, California. I doubt this book would have been written without this man's teaching that formed an important part of my foundational faith.

Mel Bennett was my pastor for nearly twenty years. His generosity in allowing me to use Calvary Temple's audio equipment to start the world's first Christian podcast was certainly a key to beginning the career that has brought me to the place where I became aware of the need for this book.

I have learned much about steadfast, rock solid integrity from my current pastor, Steve O'Brien. Since he is also my brother-in-law, I have been blessed and inspired as I see that he lives his life with consistency. The man in the pulpit is the same man at home.

So many other people have contributed to this book, as they have touched my life in important ways. Here are but a few of them: Rip and JoAnn Collins, Mark Beebout, Randy Collins, Ron Ploof, Craig Patchett, James Cooper, Bryan Duncan, and Allen P. Johnston. I am unspeakably grateful that God brought each of these incredible people into my life at just the right times. Their friendship and example changed my life.

Pronunciation Key

a = h**a**t	eye = **eye**ball	n = **n**ew	th = **th**in
ah = f**a**ther	f = **f**arm	o = m**o**del	uh = **a**bout
air = sh**are**	g = **g**ive	oh = sl**ow**	uhr = h**er**
ay = s**ay**	h = **h**ear	oi = b**oy**	v = **v**ictor
aw = l**aw**	i = p**i**ck	oo = s**oo**n	w = **w**orthy
b = **b**all	ih = p**i**ck	or = f**or**	y = **y**ellow
ch = **ch**air	im = h**im**	ou = **ou**nce	ye = sk**y**
d = **d**og	ite = k**ite**	p = **p**ony	z = **z**oo
e = l**e**t	j = **j**udge	r = **r**ose	zh = vi**si**on
eh = l**e**t	k = **k**ing	s = **s**un	
ee = s**ee**d	l = **l**amb	sh = **sh**ine	
ew = f**ew**	m = **m**an	t = **t**oy	

Emphasized syllables are in ALL CAPS. Where there are two emphasized syllables in a word, the syllable with greater emphasis is in **BOLD CAPS**.

Example: Mediterranean: MED-i-tuh-**RAY**-nee-uhn

.

A

Aalar: AY-uh-luhr

Aaron: AIR-uhn

Aaronic: air-ON-ick

Aaronite: AIR-uh-nite

Aasbai: ay-AZ-bye

Abacuc: AB-uh-kuhk

Abaddon: uh-BAD-uhn

Abadias: AB-uh-**DYE**-uhs

Abagtha: uh-BAG-thuh

Abana: AB-uh-nuh

Abanah: AB-uh-nuh

Abaran: AB-uh-ruhn

Abarim: AB-uh-rim

Abaron: AB-uh-ron

Abba: AB-uh or AH-buh

Abbas: AH-buhs

Abda: AB-duh

Abdeel: AB-dee-uhl

Abdemelech: ab-DEM-uh-lek

Abdenago: ab-DEN-uh-goh

Abdi: AB-dye

Abdias: ab-DYE-uhs

Abdiel: AB-dee-uhl

Abdon: AB-duhn

Abed: AY-bed

Abed-nego: uh-BED-neh-go

Abednego: uh-BED-neh-go

Abel: AY-buhl

Abela: ay-BEL-uh

Abel Beth Maacah: AY-buhl-beth-**MAY**-uh-kuh

Abel Bethmaacah: AY-buhl-beth-**MAY**-uh-kuh

Abel Beth Maachah: AY-buhl-beth-**MAY**-uh-kuh

Abel-beth-maacah: AY-buhl-beth-**MAY**-uh-kuh

Abel-beth-maachah: AY-buhl-beth-**MAY**-uh-kuh

Abelbethmaacah: AY-buhl-beth-**MAY**-uh-kuh

Abeldomum: AY-buhl-**DOH**-muhm

Abel Keramim: AY-buhl-**KAIR**-uh-mim

Abel-keramim: AY-buhl-**KAIR**-uh-mim

Abelkeramim: AY-buhl-**KAIR**-uh-mim

Abelmahula: AY-buhl-meh-**HOO**-luh

Abel Maim: AY-buhl-**MAY**-im

Abel-maim: AY-buhl-**MAY**-im

Abelmaim: AY-buhl-**MAY**-im

Abel Meholah: AY-buhl-meh-**HOH**-luh

Abel-meholah: AY-buhl-meh-**HOH**-luh

Abelmeholah: AY-buhl-meh-**HOH**-luh

Abelmehula: AY-buhl-meh-**YOO**-luh

Abelmeula: AY-buhl-meh-**YOO**-luh

Abel Mizraim: AY-buhl-**MIZ**-ray-im

Abel-mizraim: AY-buhl-**MIZ**-ray-im

Abelmizraim: AY-buhl-**MIZ**-ray-im

Abel Shittim: AY-buhl-**SHIT**-im

Abel-shittim: AY-buhl-**SHIT**-im

Abelshittim: AY-buhl-**SHIT**-im

Abenboen: AB-un-**BOH**-uhn

Abes: AY-bez

Abesalom: AB-suh-lom

Abesan: AB-san

Abessalom: uh-BIS-uh-luhm

Abez: AY-bez

Abi: AY-bye

Abia: uh-BY-uh

Abiah: uh-BY-uh

Abi-albon: AY-bye-**AL**-buhn

Abialbon: AY-bye-**AL**-buhn

Abiam: uh-BYE-uhm

Abiasaph: uh-BYE-uh-saf

Abiathar: uh-BYE-uh-thahr

Abib: AY-bib

Abibaal: AY-bye-**BAY**-uhl

Abida: uh-BYE-duh

Abidah: uh-BYE-duh

Abidan: uh-BYE-duhn

Abiel: AY-bee-uhl

Abi-ezer: AY-bye-**EE**-zuhr

Abiezer: AY-bye-**EE**-zuhr

Abi-ezrite: AY-bye-**EZ**-rite

Abiezrite: AY-bye-**EZ**-rite

Abigabaon: AY-bye-**GAB**-ay-uhn

Abigail: AB-eh-gayl

Abigal: AB-uh-gal

Abihaiel: AB-uh-hayl

Abihail: AB-uh-hayl

Abihu: uh-BYE-hew

Abihud: uh-BYE-huhd

Abijah: uh-BYE-juh

Abijam: uh-BYE-juhm

Abilene: AB-uh-**LEE**-nee

Abimael: uh-BIM-ay-uhl

Abimelech: uh-BIM-uh-lek

Abinadab: uh-BIN-uh-dab

Abiner: AB-uh-nuhr

Abinoam: uh-BIN-oh-uhm

Abinoem: uh-BIN-oh-uhm

Abiram: uh-BY-ruhm

Abiron: uh-BYE-ruhn

Abisag: AB-uh-sag

Abisai: uh-BYE-sye

Abisei: AB-uh-**SEE**-eye

Abishag: AB-uh-shag

Abishai: uh-BYE-shy

Abishalom: uh-BISH-uh-luhm

Abishua: uh-BISH-oo-uh

Abishur: uh-BYE-shuhr

Abisue: uh-BYE-soo-uh

Abisum: uh-BYE-suhm

Abisur: uh-BYE-suhr

Abital: uh-BYE-tuhl

Abitob: uh-BYE-tuhb

Abitub: uh-BYE-tuhb

Abiu: uh-BYE-yoo

Abiud: uh-BYE-uhd

Ablesatim: AY-buhl-**SAT**-im

Abner: AB-nuhr

Abobus: uh-BOH-buhs

Abubus: uh-BOO-buhs

Abraham: AY-bruh-ham

Abram: AY-bruhm

Abron: AY-bruhn

Abronah: uh-BROH-nuh

Absalom: AB-suh-luhm

Abshai: AB-shy

Abubus: uh-BOO-buhs

Acacia: uh-KAY-shuh

Acatan: AK-uh-tan

Acbor: AK-bohr

Accad: AK-add

Accain: AK-ayn

Accaron: AK-uh-ruhn

Acces: AK-es

Accho: AK-oh

Acco: AK-oh

Accos: AK-oz

Accoz: AK-oz

Accronite: AK-ron-ite

Accub: AK-kuhb

Aceldama: uh-KEL-duh-muh

Achab: AY-kab

Achad: AY-kad

Achaia: uh-KAY-uh

Achaicus: uh-KAY-uh-kuhs

Achan: AY-kan

Achar: AY-kahr

Achaz: AY-kaz

Achazib: AK-uh-zib

Achbor: AK-bohr

Achia: uh-KYE-uh

Achiacharus: AK-yuh-**KAY**-ruhs

Achias: uh-KYE-uhs

Achim: AY-kim

Achimaas: AY-kuh-**MAY**-uhs

Achiman: uh-KIM-muhn

Achimelech: uh-KIM-uh-lek

Achimoth: uh-KIM-muhth

Achinoam: uh-KIN-oh-am

Achior: AY-kee-ohr

Achis: AY-kis

Achish: AY-kish

Achitob: AK-uh-tahb

Achitophel: uh-KIT-oh-fel

Achmetha: AK-muh-thuh

Achobor: AK-bar

Achor: AY-kohr

Achsa: AK-suh

Achsah: AK-suh

Achsaph: AK-saf

Achshaph: AK-shaf

Achzib: AK-zib

Achziba: AK-zib

Acipha: uh-SYE-fuh

Acitho: AS-uh-thoh

Acraba: AK-ruh-buh

Acrabathane: AK-ruh-**BATH**-uh-nee

Acrabattene: AK-ruh-**BAT**-uh-nee

Acrabbim: uh-KRAB-im

Acron: AK-ruhn

Acropolis: uh-KRAH-poh-lis

Acsah: AK-suh

Acshaph: AK-shaf

Acua: uh-KEW-uh

Acub: AY-kuhb

Aczib: AK-zib

Ada: AY-duh

Adad: AY-dad

Adada: AD-uh-duh

Adadah: AD-uh-duh

Adadremmon: AY-dad-**RIM**-uhn

Adah: AY-duh

Adaiah: uh-DYE-uh

Adaias: uh-DYE-uhs

Adalia: uh-DAY-lee-uh

Adam: AD-uhm

Adama: AD-uh-muh

Adamah: AD-uh-muh

Adami: AD-uhm-eye

Adami Nekeb: AD-uh-my-**NEE**-kehb

Adami-nekeb: AD-uh-my-**NEE**-kehb

Adaminekeb: AD-uh-my-**NEE**-kehb

Adan: AY-duhn

Adar: AY-dahr

Adarezer: AY-dahr-**EE**-zuhr

Adarsa: uh-DAHR-suh

Adasa: AD-uh-suh

Adazer: AD-uh-suhr

Adbeel: AD-bee-uhl

Addan: AD-uhn

Addar: AD-dahr

Addi: AD-eye

Addo: AD-oh

Addon: AD-uhn

Addus: AD-us

Adeodatus: uh-DAY-oh-**DAT**-us

Ader: AY-duhr

Adiada: uh-DYE-uh-duh

Adida: AD-uh-duh

Adiel: AD-ee-el

Adin: AY-din

Adina: AD-uh-nuh

Adino: AD-uh-noh

Adinus: uh-DYE-nuhs

Adithaim: AD-eh-**THAY**-im

Adlai: AD-lye

Admah: AD-muh

Admatha: ad-MAY-thuh

Admin: AD-min

Adna: AD-nuh

Adnah: AD-nuh

Adom: AD-uhm

Adommin: uh-DAHM-in

Adonai: AD-oh-**NYE**

Adonay: AD-oh-**NYE**

Adonias: AD-oh-**NYE**-us

Adonibezec: uh-DOH-nye-**BEE**-zek

Adoni-bezek: uh-DOH-nye-**BEE**-zek

Adonibezek: uh-DOH-nye-**BEE**-zek

Adonijah: AD-uh-**NYE**-juh

Adonikam: AD-uh-**NYE**-kuhm

Adoniram: AD-uh-**NYE**-ruhm

Adonisedec: uh-DOH-nye-**ZEE**-dek

Adoni-zedek: uh-DOH-nye-**ZEE**-dek

Adonizedek: uh-DOH-nye-**ZEE**-dek

Ador: AY-dohr

Adora: uh-DOH-ruh

Adoraim: AD-uh-**RAY**-im

Adoram: uh-DOH-ruhm

Adramelech: uh-DRAM-uh-lek

Adram-melech: uh-DRAM-muh-lek

Adrammelech: uh-DRAM-uh-lek

Adrammelek: uh-DRAM-uh-lek

Adramyttian: AD-ruh-**MIT**-ee-uhn

Adramyttium: AD-ruh-**MIT**-ee-uhm

Adria: AY-dree-uh

Adriatic: AY-dree-**AT**-ick

Adriel: AY-dree-uhl

Aduel: uh-DEW-uhl

Adullam: uh-DUHL-uhm

Adullamite: uh-DUHL-uh-mite

Adummim: uh-DUHM-im

Aduram: uh-DEW-ruhm

Aen: eyen

Aeneas: eh-NEE-uhs

Aenon: EE-nuhn

Aesora: eh-SOH-ruh

Agaba: AG-uh-buh

Agabus: AG-uh-buhs

Agade: uh-GAH-dee

Agag: AY-gag

Agagite: AG-uh-gite

Agar: AY-gahr

Agarai: AG-uh-rye

Agaren: AG-uh-ren

Agarite: AG-uh-rite

Age: AY-gee

Agee: AY-gee

Aggaeus: AG-ee-uhs

Aggeus: AG-ee-uhs

Aggi: AG-eye

Aggith: AG-ith

Agia: AY-gee-uh

Agrippa: uh-GRIP-uh

Agur: AY-guhr

Ahab. AY-hab

Ahalab: uh-HAH-lab

Ahara: uh-HAIR-uh

Aharah: uh-HAIR-uh

Aharehel: uh-HAHR-hel

Aharhel: uh-HAHR-hel

Ahasabi: uh-HAS-uh-bye

Ahasai: uh-HAY-sye

Ahasbai: uh-HAZ-bye

Ahashtarite: uh-HASH-tuh-rite

Ahashuerus: uh-HASH-yoo-**AIR**-uhs

Ahasthari: uh-HAS-tuh-rye

Ahasuerus: uh-HAS-yoo-**AIR**-uhs

Ahava: uh-HAY-vuh

Ahaz: AY-haz

Ahaziah: AY-huh-**ZYE**-uh

Ahban: AH-ban

Aher: AY-huhr

Ahi: AY-hye

Ahia: uh-HYE-uh

Ahiah: uh-HYE-uh

Ahialon: uh-HYE-luhn

Ahiam: uh-HYE-uhm

Ahian: uh-HYE-uhn

Ahicam: uh-HYE-kuhm

Ahiezer: AY-hye-**EE**-zuhr

Ahihud: uh-HYE-huhd

Ahijah: uh-HYE-juh

Ahikam: uh-HYE-kuhm

Ahikar: uh-HYE-kahr

Ahilud: uh-HYE-luhd

Ahimaaz: uh-HIM-uh-az

Ahiman: uh-HYE-muhn

Ahimelech: uh-HIM-uh-lek

Ahimoth: uh-HYE-muhth

Ahinadab: uh-HIN-uh-dab

Ahinoam: uh-HIN-oh-uhm

Ahio: uh-HYE-oh

Ahion: uh-HYE-uhn

Ahiqar: uh-HYE-kahr

Ahira: uh-HYE-ruh

Ahiram: uh-HYE-ruhm

Ahiramite: uh-HYE-ruh-mite

Ahisahar: uh-HIS-uh-har

Ahisamach: uh-HIS-uh-mak

Ahisar: uh-HYE-sahr

Ahishahar: uh-HISH-uh-hahr

Ahishar: uh-HYE-shahr

Ahithophel: uh-HITH-uh-fel

Ahitob: uh-HYE-tob

Ahitub: uh-HYE-tuhb

Ahiu: uh-HYE-uh

Ahiud: uh-HYE-uhd

Ahlab: AH-lab

Ahlai: AH-lye

Ahoah: uh-HOH-uh

Ahobban: uh-HOH-ban

Ahod: uh-HOHD

Ahoe: uh-HOH-uh

Ahoh: uh-HOH

Ahohi: uh-HOH-hye

Ahohite: uh-HOH-hite

Ahotite: uh-HOH-tite

Ahola: uh-HOH-luh

Aholah: uh-HOH-luh

Aholiab: uh-HOH-lee-ab

Aholibah: uh-HOH-leh-buh

Aholibamah: uh-HOH-leh-**BAH**-muh

Ahumai: uh-HEW-mye

Ahuzam: uh-HOO-zuhm

Ahuzzam: uh-HUH-zuhm

Ahuzzath: uh-HUH-zath

Ahzai: AH-zye

Ai: AY-eye or eye

Aia: AY-yuh

Aiah: AY-yuh

Aialon: AY-uh-lahn

Aiath: AY-yath

Aija: AY-juh

Aijalon: AY-juh-lahn

Aijeleth: AY-juh-leth

Aijeleth Shahar: AY-juh-leth-SHAY-hahr

Aijeleth-shahar: AY-juh-leth-SHAY-hahr

Aila: AY-luh

Ailath: AY-lath

Ain: ayn

ain: AH-yin

Aion: AY-on

Airus: AY-ruhs

Ajah: AY-juh

Ajalon: AJ-uh-lon

Akan: AY-kan

Akeldama: uh-KEL-duh-muh

Akim: AY-kim

Akkad: AK-ad

Akkub: AK-uhb

Akrabattene: AK-ruh-**BAT**-uh-nee

Akrabbim: uh-KRAB-im

Alamath: AL-uh-muhth

Alammelech: uh-LAM-uh-lek

Alamoth: AL-uh-moth

Alcimus: AL-seh-muss

Alema: AL-ee-muh

Alemeth: AL-uh-muhth

aleph: AH-leff

Alexander: AL-ig-**ZAN**-duhr

Alexandria: AL-ig-**ZAN**-dree-uh

Alexandrian: AL-ig-**ZAN**-dree-uhn

Aliah: AL-ee-uh

Aliam: uh-LYE-um

Alian: AL-ee-an

Alicarnassus: AL-eh-kahr-**NAS**-uhs

Alima: AL-ee-muh

Allammelech: uh-LAM-uh-lek

alleluia: AL-eh-**LOO**-yuh

Allemeth: AL-uh-meth

Allom: AL-ahm

Allon: AL-ahn

Allon Bachuth: AL-uhn-**BAK**-uhth

Allon-bachuth: AL-uhn-**BAK**-uhth

Allonbacuth: AL-uhn-**BAK**-uhth

Allon-bacuth: AL-uhn-**BAK**-uhth

Allon Bacuth: AL-uhn-**BAK**-uhth

Allon Bakuth: AL-uhn-**BAK**-uhth

Almath: AL-uh-meth

Almodad: al-MOH-dad

Almon: AL-mun

Almon Diblathaim: AL-muhn-DIB-luh-**THAY**-im

Almon-diblathaim: AL-muhn-DIB-luh-**THAY**-im

Almondiblathaim: AL-muhn-DIB-luh-**THAY**-im

Almugwood: AL-muhg-wood

Alnathan: al-NAY-thuhn

Aloth: AY-loth

Alpha: AL-fuh

Alphaeus: al-FEE-uhs

Alpheus: al-FEE-uhs

Altaneus: al-tuh-NEE-uhs

Al-taschit: al-TAS-kit

Al-taschith: al-TAS-kith

Altashheth: al-TAHSH-heth

Alummelech: uh-LUHM-uh-lek

Alus: AY-luhsh

Alush: AY-luhsh

Alva: AL-vuh

Alvah: AL-vuh

Alvan: AL-vuhn

Amaad: AY-mad

Amad: AY-mad

Amadatha: AM-uh-**DAY**-thuh

Amai: AHM-rye

Amal: AY-muhl

Amalec: AM-uh-lek

Amalecite: uh-MAL-uh-kite

Amalek: AM-uh-lek

Amalekite: uh-MAL-uh-kite

Amam: AY-mahm

Aman: AY-muhn

Amana: uh-MAY-nuh

Amariah: AM-er-**EYE**-uh

Amarias: AM-er-**EYE**-uhs

Amasa: uh-MAY-suh

Amasai: uh-MAY-sye

Amashai: uh-MASH-eye

Amashsai: uh-MASH-sye

Amasi: uh-MAY-sye

Amasiah: AM-uh-**SYE**-uh

Amasias: AM-uh-**SYE**-uhs

Amath: AY-muhth

Amatheis: AM-uh-**THEE**-uhs

Amathi: uh-MATH-eye

Amathis: AM-uh-this

Amaw: AY-maw

Amawite: AY-maw-ite

Amaziah: AM-uh-**ZYE**-uh

Amelech: AM-uh-lek

Amen: AH-mun

amen: AY-**MEN** or ah-MEN

Ami: AY-my

Amiel: AM-ee-uhl

Aminadab: uh-MIN-uh-dab

Amital: uh-MIT-tuhl

Amittai: uh-MIT-eye

Amizabad: uh-MIZ-uh-bad

Amma: AM-uh

Ammah: AM-uh

Ammaus: uh-MAY-uhs

Ammi: AM-eye

Ammidian: uh-MID-ee-uhn

Ammidoi: AM-uh-doi

Ammiel: AM-ee-uhl

Ammihel: AM-ee-hel

Ammihud: uh-MY-huhd

Ammihur: uh-MY-huhr

Amminadab: uh-MIN-uh-dab

Amminadib: uh-MIN-uh-dib

Ammi-nadib: AM-eye-**NAY**-dib

Ammisaddai: AM-eh-**SAD**-eye

Ammishaddai: AM-eh-**SHAD**-eye

Ammiud: uh-MY-uhd

Ammizabad: uh-MIZ-uh-bad

Ammon: AM-muhn

Ammonite: AM-uh-nite

Ammonitess: AM-uh-nite-ess

Amnon: AM-non

Amok: AY-mahk

Amon: AM-uhn

Amona: uh-MOH-nuh

Amorite: AM-uh-rite

Amorrhite: AM-or-hite

Amos: AY-muhs

Amosa. uh-MOH-zuh

Amoz: AY-muhz

Amphipolis: am-FIP-uh-lis

Amplias: AM-plee-uhs

Ampliatus: AM-pleh-**AY**-tuhs

Amram: AM-ram

Amramite: AM-ruh-mite

Amraphel: AM-ruh-fel

Amri: AM-rye

Amthar: AM-thahr

Amzi: AM-zye

Ana: AY-nuh

Anab: AY-nab

Anael: AN-ay-uhl

Anah: AY-nuh

Anaharath: uh-NAY-huh-rath

Anaiah: uh-NAY-uh

Anak: AY-nak

Anakim: AN-uh-kim

Anakite: AN-uh-kite

Anam: AY-nuhm

Anamelech: uh-NAM-uh-leck

Anamim: AN-uh-mim

Anamite: AN-uh-mite

Anammelech: uh-NAM-uh-leck

Anan: AY-nuhn

Anani: uh-NAY-nye

Ananiah: AN-uh-**NYE**-uh

Ananias: AN-uh-**NYE**-uhs

Ananiel: uh-NAN-ee-uhl

Anasib: AN-uh-sib

Anath: AY-nath

anathema: uh-NATH-eh-muh

Anathoth: AN-uh-thahth

Anathothia: AN-thoh-**THYE**-uh

Anathothite: AN-uh-thoh-thite

Andrew: AN-droo

Andronicus: an-DRAHN-eh-kuhs

Anduram: an-DOR-um

Anem: AY-num

Aner: AY-ner

Anethothite: AN-uh-thoh-thite

Anetothite: AN-uh-toh-thite

Angle: AN-guhl

Ani: UN-eye

Aniam: uh-NYE-uhm

Anim: AY-nim

Anna: AN-uh

Annaas: AN-ay-uhs

Annan: AN-uhn

Annas: AN-uhs

Annias: uh-NYE-uhs

Anniuth: uh-NYE-uhth

Annunus: AN-yoo-nuhs

Annuus: AN-yoo-uhs

Anob: AY-nuhb

Anos: AY-nahs

Anthothijah: AN-thoh-**THYE**-juh

Antichrist: AN-tee-kryst

Anti-lebanon: AN-tee-**LEB**-uh-nuhn

Antilebanon: AN-tee-**LEB**-uh-nuhn

antimony: **AN**-tuh-MOH-nee

Antioch: AN-tee-ahk

Antiocha: an-TYE-uh-kuh

Antiochian: AN-tee-**AHK**-ee-uhn

Antiochis: an-TYE-uh-kis

Antiochus: an-TYE-uh-kuhs

Antipas: AN-tee-puhs

Antipater: an-TIP-uh-tuhr

Antipatris: an-TIP-uh-tris

Antothijah: AN-toh-**THYE**-juh

Antothite: AN-tuh-thite

Anub: AY-nuhb

Anus: AY-nuhs

Aod: AY-uhd

Apadno: uh-PED-noo

Apame: uh-PAY-mee

Apelles: uh-PEL-eez

Aphairema: uh-FAIR-uh-muh

Aphara: uh-PAY-ruh

Apharsachite: uh-FAHR-suh-kite

Apharsathcite: uh-FAHR-suhth-kite

Apharsite: uh-FAHR-site

Aphec: AY-fek

Apheca: uh-FEE-kuh

Aphek: AY-fek

Aphekah: uh-FEE-kuh

Apherema: uh-FAIR-uh-muh

Apherra: uh-FAIR-uh

Aphia: uh-FYE-uh

Aphiah: uh-FYE-uh

Aphik: AY-fick

Aphrah: AF-ruh

Aphses: AF-seez

Aphuthite: uh-PEW-thite

Apis: AY-piss

Apocalypse: uh-PAHK-uh-lips

Apollonia: AP-uh-**LOH**-nee-uh

Apollonius: APP-uh-**LOH**-nee-uhs

Apollophanes: APP-uh-**LOFF**-uh-neez

Apollos: uh-PAHL-uhs

Apollyon: uh-PAHL-yuhn

apostasy: uh-PAHS-tuh-see

apostate: uh-PAHS-tayt

apostle: uh-PAHS-uhl

apostolic: AP-uh-**STAH**-lick

Appaim: AP-ay-im

Apphaim: AP-ay-im

Apphia: AF-ee-uh

Apphus: AF-uhs

Appian: AP-ee-uhn

Appii: AP-ee-eye

Appius: AP-ee-uhs

Aqaba: AH-kuh-bah

Aqabah: AH-kuh-bah

Aquila: AK-weh-luh

Ar: ahr

Ara: AIR-uh or AY-ruh

Araas: AHR-as

Arab: AIR-uhb

Arabah: AIR-uh-buh

Arabattine: AIR-uh-**BAT**-uh-nee

Arabella: AHR-uh-**bell**-uh

Arabia: uh-RAY-bee-uh

Arabian: uh-RAY-bee-uhn

Arabim: AIR-uh-bim

Arach: EE-rek

Arachite: AHR-uh-kite

Aracite: AHR-uh-kite

Arad: AIR-ad or AY-rad

Arada: uh-RAY-duh

Aradian: ahr-OD-ee-un

Aradite: AIR-uh-dite

Arados: AIR-uh-duhs

Aradus: AIR-uh-duhs

Arah: AY-ruh

Aram: AIR-uhm

Arama: uh-RAY-muh

Aramaic: AIR-uh-**MAY**-ick

Aramean: AIR-uh-**MEE**-uhn

Aramitess. **AIR**-uh-MY-tess

Aram Maacah: AIR-uhm-**MAY**-uh-kuh

Aram-maacah: AIR-uhm-**MAY**-uh-kuh

Arammaacah: AIR-uhm-**MAY**-uh-kuh

Aram Naharaim: AIR-uhm-nay-huh-**RAY**-im

Aram-naharaim: AIR-uhm-nay-huh-**RAY**-im

Aram-Zobah: AIR-uhm-**ZOH**-buh

Aran: AIR-an or AY-run

Arapha: AHR-ah-fuh

Ararat: AIR-uh-rat

Arari: uh-RAH-rye

Ararite: AIR-uh-rite

Araunah: uh-RAH-nuh

Arba: AHR-buh

Ar-baal: ahr-BAY-uhl

Arbah: AHR-buh

Arbathite: AHR-buh-thite

Arbatis: ahr-BAT-is

Arbatta: ahr-BAT-uh

Arbattis: ahr-BAT-is

Arbe: AHR-buh

Arbela: ahr-BEE-luh

Arbi: AHR-bye

Arbite: AHR-bite

Arbonai: ahr-BOH-nye

archangel: ahrk-ayn-juhl

Archelaus: AHR-kuh-**LAY**-uhs

Archevite: AHR-kuh-vite

Archi: AHR-kye

Archippus: ahr-KIP-uhs

Archite: AHR-kite

Arcturus: ahrk-TOOR-uhs

Ard: ahrd

Ardat: AHR-dat

Ardath: AHR-dath

Ardite: AHR-dite

Ardon: AHR-don

Arebba: uh-RAB-buh

Arecon: uh-RAK-uhn

Aree: AY-ree

Areli: uh-REE-lye

Arelite: uh-REE-lite

Areopagite: AIR-ee-**AHP**-uh-gite

Areopagus: AIR-ee-**AHP**-uh-guhs

Ares: AIR-eez

Aretas: AIR-uh-tuhs

Areuna: uh-ROO-nuh

Areus: AIR-ee-uhs

Argob: AHR-gob

Ariarathes: AIR-ee-uh-**RAY**-theez

Ariarthes: AIR-ee-**AHR**-theez

Ariathes: AIR-ee-**AY**-theez

Aridai: AIR-uh-dye

Aridatha: AIR-uh-**DAY**-thuh

Arie: AIR-ee-uh

Arieh: AIR-ee-uh

Ariel: AIR-ee-uhl

Arimathaea: AIR-uh-muh-**THEE**-uh

Arimathea: AIR-uh-muh-**THEE**-uh

Arioch: AIR-ee-ahck

Arisai: AIR-uh-sye

Aristarchus: AIR-eh-**STAHR**-kuhs

Aristobolus: AIR-is-**TAHB**-uh-luhs

Aristobulus: AIR-is-**TAHB**-yuh-luhs

Arius: AIR-ee-uhs

Arkite: AHR-kite

Armageddon: AHR-muh-**GEHD**-uhn

Armenia: ahr-MEE-nee-uh

Armon: AHR-muhn

Armoni: ahr-MOH-nye

Arna: AHR-nuh

Arnan: AHR-nuhn

Arni: AHR-nye

Arnon: AHR-nuhn

Arod: AIR-ahd

Arodi: AIR-uh-dye

Arodite: AIR-uh-dite

Aroer: uh-ROH-uhr

Aroerite: uh-ROH-uh-rite

Arom: AIR-uhm

Arorite: uh-ROH-uh-rite

Arpachshad: ahr-PAK-shad

Arpad: AHR-pad

Arphad: AHR-fad

Arphaxad: ahr-FAX-ad

Arsa: AHR-zuh

Arsaces: AHR-suh-seez

Arsareth: AHR-suh-reth

Arsinoe: ahr-SIN-oh-ee

Artaxerxes: AHR-tuh-**ZUHRK**-seez

Artemas: AHR-tuh-muhs

Artemis: AHR-tuh-mis

artificer: are-TIFF-uh-suhr

Arubboth: uh-RUH-bahth

Aruboth: uh-ROO-bahth

Arum: AY-ruhm

Arumah: uh-ROO-mah

Arvad: AHR-vad

Arvadite: AHR-vuh-dite

Arza: AHR-zuh

Arzareth: AHR-zuh-rehth

Asa: AY-suh

Asadias: AS-uh-**DYE**-uhs

Asael: AS-ay-uhl

Asahel: AS-uh-hell

Asahiah: AS-uh-**HYE**-uh

Asaia: uh-ZAY-uh

Asaiah: uh-ZAY-uh

Asaias: uh-ZAY-uhs

Asalelphuni: AS-uh-lel-**FUH**-nye

Asan: AY-suhn

Asana: uh-SAH-nuh

Asaph: AY-saf

Asaramel: uh-SAIR-uh-mel

Asareel: uh-SAIR-ee-uhl

Asarel: AS-uh-rel

Asarelah: AS-uh-**REE**-luh

Asarhaddon: AY-sahr-**HAD**-duhn

Asarmoth: uh-SAIR-moth

Asbel: AS-bel

Ascalon: AS-kuh-lahn

Ascalonite: as-KAL-uh-nite

Ascenez: AS-ken-az

Aseas: AS-ee-uhs

Asebebia: AS-uh-**BEE**-bee-uh

Asebia: uh-SEE-bee-uh

Asedoth: AZ-duhth

Asel: AY-zuhl

Asem: AY-zuhm

Asemona: AZ-muh-nuh

Asena: AZ-nuh

Asenath: AS-uh-nath

Aser: AY-suhr

Aserer: AY-suh-ruhr

Asergadda: AY-zuhr-GAD-duh

Ashan: AY-shuhn

Asharelah: ASH-uh-**REE**-luh

Ashbea: ASH-bee-uh

Ashbel: ASH-bel

Ashbelite: ASH-buh-lite

Ashchenaz: ASH-kuh-naz

Ashdod: ASH-dahd

Ashdodite: ASH-duh-dite

Ashdothite: ASH-duh-thite

Ashdoth-pisgah: ASH-doth-**PIZ**-guh

Asher: ASH-uhr

Asherah: uh-SHEER-uh

Asherim: uh-SHEER-ehm

Asherite: ASH-uh-rite

Asheroth: uh-SHEER-ahth

Ashhur: ASH-uhr

Ashima: uh-SHY-muh

Ashimah: uh-SHY-muh

Ashkalon: ASH-kuh-lahn

Ashkelon: ASH-kuh-lahn

Ashkelonite: ASH-kuh-luh-nite

Ashkenaz: ASH-kuh-naz

Ashnah: ASH-nuh

Ashpenaz: ASH-puh-naz

Ashriel: ASH-ree-uhl

Ashtaroth: ASH-tuh-rahth

Ashterath: ASH-tuh-rahth

Ashterathite: ASH-tuh-ruh-thite

Ashteroth: ASH-tuh-rahth

Ashteroth Karnaim: ASH-tuh-rahth-kahr-NAY-im

Ashteroth-karnaim: ASH-tuh-rahth-kahr-NAY-im

Ashterothkarnaim: ASH-tuh-rahth-kahr-NAY-im

Ashtoreth: ASH-tuh-reth

Ashur: ASH-uhr

Ashurbanipal: ASH-uhr-**BAN**-uh-puhl

Ashuri: ASH-uhr-eye

Ashurite: ASH-uhr-ite

Ashvath: ASH-vath

Asia: AY-zhuh

Asian: AY-zhuhn

Asiarch: AY-zhee-ahrk

Asibias: AS-uh-**BYE**-uhs

Asidean: AS-uh-**DEE**-uhn

Asiel: AS-ee-el

Asima: uh-SHY-muh

Asiongaber: AY-zee-ahn-**GAY**-buhr

Asipha: uh-SIF-uh

Asir: AZ-uhr

Askalon: AS-kuh-lahn

Askelon: AS-kuh-lahn

Asmodeus: AZ-moh-**DEE**-uhs

Asnah: AS-nuh

Asnapper: as-NAP-uhr

Asom: AY-suhm

Asor: AY-zore

Asoth: AS-ahth

Aspalathus: as-PAL-uh-thuhs

Aspatha: as-PAY-thuh

Asphar: AS-fahr

Aspharasus: as-FAIR-uh-suhs

Asphenez: ASH-puh-naz

Asrael: us-RAY-uhl

Asriel: AZ-ree-uhl

Asrielite: AZ-ree-uh-lite

Assabias: AZ-uh-**BYE**-uhs

Assalimoth: uh-SAL-uh-mahth

Assanias: AS-uh-**NYE**-uhs

Assedim: uh-ZID-im

Assem: AY-sem

Asser: AS-uhr

Asshur: AS-huhr

Asshurim: AS-huh-rim

Asshurite: AS-huh-rite

Assia: uh-**SYE**-uh

Assidean: AS-uh-**DEE**-uhn

Assir: AZ-uhr

Assos: AZ-ahs

Assur: AS-uhr

Assurbanipal: AS-uhr-**BAN**-uh-puhl

Assurim: az-YOO-rim

Assyria: uh-SEER-ee-uh

Assyrian: uh-SEER-ee-uhn

Astaroth: AS-tuh-rahth

Astarothite: AS-tuh-rahth-ite

Astarte: as-TAHR-tee

Astarthe: as-TAHR-tee

Astath: AS-tath

Astharoth: ASH-tuhr-ahth

Astyages: uh-STY-uh-jeez

Asuerus: AZH-yoo-**AIR**-uhs

Asuppim: uh-SUHP-im

Asur: AY-suhr

Aswan: as-WAHN

Asyncritus: uh-SIN-kreh-tuhs

Atad: AY-tad

Atara: AT-uh-ruh

Atarah: AT-uh-ruh

Atargatis: uh-TAHR-guh-tis

Ataroth: AT-uh-rahth

Ataroth Adar: AT-uh-rahth-**AD**-uhr

Ataroth-adar: AT-uh-rahth-**AD**-uhr

Ataroth-addar: AT-uh-rahth-**AD**-uhr

Atarothaddar: AT-uh-rahth-**AD**-uhr

Atbash: AT-bash

Ater: AY-tuhr

Aterezias: uh-TAIR-uh-**ZYE**-uhs

Athach: AY-thak

Athaiah: uh-THAY-uh

Athalia: ATH-uh-**LYE**-uh

Athaliah: ATH-uh-**LYE**-uh

Athanai: ATH-uh-nye

Atharias: ATH-uh-**RYE**-uhs

Atharim: ATH-uh-rim

Athbash: ATH-bash

Athenian: uh-THEE-nee-uhn

Athenobius: ATH-uh-**NOH**-bee-us

Athens: ATH-ehnz

Athlai: ATH-lye

Athmatha: ATH-muh-thuh

Athor: ATH-uhr

Atipha: uh-TYE-fuh

Atroth: AT-rahth

Atroth beth Joab: AT-rahth-beth-**JOH**-ab

Atroth-beth-joab: AT-rahth-beth-**JOH**-ab

Atrothbethjoab: AT-rahth-beth-**JOH**-ab

Atroth Shophan: AT-rahth-**SHOH**-fan

Atroth-shophan: AT-rahth-**SHOH**-fan

Atrothshophan: AT-rahth-**SHOH**-fan

Attai: AT-eye

Attalia: AT-uh-**LYE**-uh

Attalus: AT-uh-luhs

Attharates: ATH-uh-**RAY**-teez

Attharias: ATH-uh-**RYE**-uhs

Augia: AW-jee-uh

Augusta: aw-GUHS-tuh

Augustan: aw-GUHS-tuhn

Augustus: aw-GUHS-tuhs

Auran: OR-uhn

Auranus: aw-RAY-nuhs

Ausitis: uh-ZYE-tuhs

Auteas: aw-TEE-uhs

Ava: AY-vuh

Avah: AY-vuh

Avaran: AV-uh-ran

Aven: AY-ven

Avim: AY-vim

Avite: AY-vite

Avith: AY-vith

Avva: AV-uh

Avvim: AV-im

Avvite: AV-ite

Awil-merodach: AY-vuhl-**MAIR**-uh-dak

Axa: AX-uh

Axaph: AHX-ahff

ayin: EYE-yin

Ayyah: AH-yuh

Azael: AY-zay-uhl

Azaelus: AZ-uh-**EE**-luhs

Azal: AY-zuhl

Azaliah: AZ-uh-**LYE**-uh

Azaniah: AZ-uh-**NYE**-uh

Azanotthabor: AZ-uh-nahth-**THAY**-buhr

Azaphion: uh-ZAY-fee-uhn

Azara: AZ-uh-ruh

Azarael: AZ-uh-**RAY**-uhl

Azareel: AZ-uh-**REE**-uhl

Azarel: AZ-uh-rel

Azariah: AZ-uh-**RYE**-uh

Azariahu: AZ-uh-**RYE**-uh-hew

Azarias: AZ-uh-**RYE**-uhs

Azaru: AZ-uh-roo

Azaryahu: AZ-uhr-**YAH**-hoo

Azaz: AY-zaz

Azazel: uh-ZAY-zuhl

Azaziah: AZ-uh-**ZYE**-uh

Azbai: AZ-bye

Azbazareth: az-BAZ-uh-rehth

Azbuk: AZ-buhk

Azeca: uh-ZEE-kuh

Azekah: uh-ZEE-kuh

Azel: AY-zuhl

Azem: AY-zuhm

Azephurith: uh-ZEF-uh-rihth

Azetas: uh-ZEE-tuhs

Azgad: AZ-gad

Azia: AZ-ee-uh

Aziei: AZ-uh-**EE**-eye

Aziel: AY-zee-uhl

Aziza: uh-ZYE-zuh

Azmaveth: AZ-muh-veth

Azmon: AZ-muhn

Azmoth: AZ-muhth

Aznoth Tabor: AZ-nahth-**TAY**-buhr

Aznoth-tabor: AZ-nahth-**TAY**-buhr

Aznothtabor: AZ-nahth-**TAY**-buhr

Azor: AY-zohr

Azotian: uh-ZOH-tee-uhn

Azotus: uh-ZOE-tuhs

Azriel: AZ-ree-uhl

Azrikam: AZ-ruh-kuhm

Azuba: uh-ZOO-buh

Azubah: uh-ZOO-buh

Azur: AY-zuhr

Azuran: uh-ZOO-ruhn

Azzah: AZ-uh

Azzan: AZ-uhn

Azzur: AZ-uhr

B

Baal: BAY-uhl or bah-AHL

Baala: BAY-uh-luh or BAH-uh-luh

Baalah: BAY-uh-luh or BAH-uh-luh

Baalam: BAY-uh-luhm or BAH-uh-luhm

Baalath: BAY-uh-lath or BAH-uh-lath

Baalath Beer: BAY-uh-lath-**BEE**-uhr or BAH-uh-lath-**BEE**-uhr

Baalath-beer: BAY-uh-lath-**BEE**-uhr or BAH-uh-lath-**BEE**-uhr

Baalathbeer: BAY-uh-lath-**BEE**-uhr or BAH-uh-lath-**BEE**-uhr

Baal-berith: BAY-uhl-beh-**RITH** or BAH-uhl-beh-**RITH**

Baalberith: BAY-uhl-beh-**RITH** or BAH-uhl-beh-**RITH**

Baale: BAY-uh-lee or BAH-uh-lee

Baale Judah: BAY-uh-lee-**JOO**-duh or BAH-uh-lee-**JOO**-duh

Baale-judah: BAY-uh-lee-**JOO**-duh or BAH-uh-lee-**JOO**-duh

Baalejudah: BAY-uh-lee-**JOO**-duh or BAH-uh-lee-**JOO**-duh

Baal Gad: BAY-uhl-**GAD** or BAH-uhl-**GAD**

Baal-gad: BAY-uhl-**GAD** or BAH-uhl-**GAD**

Baalgad: BAY-uhl-**GAD** or BAH-uhl-**GAD**

Baal Hamon: BAY-uhl-**HAY**-muhn or BAH-uhl-**HAY**-muhn

Baal-hamon: BAY-uhl-**HAY**-muhn or BAH-uhl-**HAY**-muhn

Baalhamon: BAY-uhl-**HAY**-muhn or BAH-uhl-**HAY**-muhn

Baal Hanan: BAY-uhl-**HAY**-nuhn or BAH-uhl-**HAY**-nuhn

Baal-hanan: BAY-uhl-**HAY**-nuhn or BAH-uhl-**HAY**-nuhn

Baalhanan: BAY-uhl-**HAY**-nuhn or BAH-uhl-**HAY**-nuhn

Baal Hazor: BAY-uhl-**HAY**-zor or BAH-uhl-**HAY**-zor

Baal-hazor: BAY-uhl-**HAY**-zor or BAH-uhl-**HAY**-zor

Baalhazor: BAY-uhl-**HAY**-zor or BAH-uhl-**HAY**-zor

Baal Hermon: BAY-uhl-**HUHR**-muhn or BAH-uhl-**HUHR**-muhn

Baal-hermon: BAY-uhl-**HUHR**-muhn or BAH-uhl-**HUHR**-muhn

Baalhermon: BAY-uhl-**HUHR**-muhn or BAH-uhl-**HUHR**-muhn

Baali: BAY-uh-lye or BAH-uh-lye

Baalia: BAY-uh-**LYE**-uh or BAH-uh-**LYE**-uh

Baaliada: BAY-uh-**LYE**-uh-duh or BAH-uh-**LYE**-uh-duh

Baalim: BAY-uh-lim or BAH-uh-lim

Baalis: BAY-uh-lis or BAH-uh-lis

Baalmaon: BAY-uhl-**MAY**-ahn or BAH-uhl-**MAY**-ahn

Baal Meon: BAY-uhl-**MEE**-ahn or BAH-uhl-**MEE**-ahn

Baal-meon: BAY-uhl-**MEE**-ahn or BAH-uhl-**MEE**-ahn

Baalmeon: BAY-uhl-**MEE**-ahn or BAH-uhl-**MEE**-ahn

Baal Peor: BAY-uhl-**PEE**-or or BAH-uhl-**PEE**-or

Baal-peor: BAY-uhl-**PEE**-or or BAH-uhl-**PEE**-or

Baalpeor: BAY-uhl-**PEE**-or or BAH-uhl-**PEE**-or

Baal Perazim: BAY-uhl-peh-**RAY**-zim or BAH-uhl-peh-**RAY**-zim

Baal-perazim: BAY-uhl-peh-**RAY**-zim or BAH-uhl-peh-**RAY**-zim

Baalperazim: BAY-uhl-peh-**RAY**-zim or BAH-uhl-peh-**RAY**-zim

Baal Pharisim: BAY-uhl-peh-**RAY**-zim or BAH-uhl-peh-**RAY**-zim

Baalpharasim: BAY-uhl-peh-**RAY**-zim or BAH-uhl-peh-**RAY**-zim

Baalsalisa: BAY-uhl-**SHAL**-ish-uh or BAH-uhl-**SHAL**-ish-uh

Baal Shalisa: BAY-uhl-**SHAL**-ish-uh or BAH-uhl-**SHAL**-ish-uh

Baal-shalisa: BAY-uhl-**SHAL**-ish-uh or BAH-uhl-**SHAL**-ish-uh

Baal Shalisah: BAY-uhl-**SHAL**-ish-uh or BAH-uhl-**SHAL**-ish-uh

Baal-shalisah: BAY-uhl-**SHAL**-ish-uh or BAH-uhl-**SHAL**-ish-uh

Baalshalisah: BAY-uhl-**SHAL**-ish-uh or BAH-uhl-**SHAL**-ish-uh

Baal Tamar: BAY-uhl-**TAY**-mahr or BAH-uhl-**TAY**-mahr

Baal-tamar: BAY-uhl-**TAY**-mahr or BAH-uhl-**TAY**-mahr

Baaltamar: BAY-uhl-**TAY**-mahr or BAH-uhl-**TAY**-mahr

Baal Thamar: BAY-uhl-**TAY**-mahr or BAH-uhl-**TAY**-mahr

Baal-thamar: BAY-uhl-**TAY**-mahr or BAH-uhl-**TAY**-mahr

Baalthamar: BAY-uhl-**TAY**-mahr or BAH-uhl-**TAY**-mahr

Baal-zebub: BAY-uhl-**ZEE**-buhb or BAH-uhl-**ZEE**-buhb

Baalzebub: BAY-uhl-**ZEE**-buhb or BAH-uhl-**ZEE**-buhb

Baalzephon: BAY-uhl-**ZEE**-fahn or BAH-uhl-**ZEE**-fahn

Baana: BAY-uh-nuh

Baanah: BAY-uh-nuh

Baanias: BAY-uh-**NYE**-uhs

Baara: BAY-uh-ruh

Baasa: BAY-uh-suh

Baaseiah: BAY-uh-**SEE**-uh

Baasha: BAY-uh-shuh

Babel: BAY-bul

Babi: BAY-bye

Babylon: BAB-uh-lahn

Babylonia: BAB-uh-**LOH**-nee-uh

Babylonian: BAB-uh-**LOH**-nee-uhn

Babylonish: BAB-uh-**LOH**-nish

Baca: BAY-kuh

Bacbacar: bak-BAK-ar

Bacchides: BAK-uh-deez

Bacchurus: bak-YOO-ruhs

Bacchus: BAK-uhs

Bacenor: buh-SEE-nor

Bachrite: BAK-rite

Bachuth: BAY-kuhth

Bacuth: BAY-kuhth

Badacer: BID-uh-kar

Badad: BEE-dad

Badan: BEE-dan

Baden: BEE-dan

Baean: BEE-uhn

Bagathan: BAG-uh-than

Bago: BAY-goh

Bagoas: buh-GOH-uhs

Bagoi: BAY-goi

Bah: bah

Baharum: buh-HAIR-uhm

Baharumite: buh-HAIR-uh-mite

Bahurim: buh-HEW-rim

Baiterus: BYE-tuh-ruhs

Baither: BYE-thuhr

Bajith: BAY-jith

Bakbakkar: bak-BAK-uhr

Bakbuk: BAK-buhk

Bakbukiah: BAK-buh-**KYE**-uh

Bakuth: BAY-kuhth

Bala: BAY-luh

Balaam: BAY-luhm

Balaan: BAY-luhn

Balaath: BAY-lath

Balac: BAY-lak

Balach: BAY-lak

Baladan: BAL-uh-duhn

Balah: BAY-luh

Balak: BAY-lak

Balamo: BAY-luh-moh

Balamon: BAL-uh-muhn

Balan: BAY-luhn

Balanan: bal-AY-nun

Balasamus: buh-LAS-uh-muhs

Balbaim: bal-BAY-im

Baldad: BAL-dad

Bale: BAY-luh

Balnuus: BAL-noo-uhs

Baloth: BAY-loth

Baltasar: bal-TAZ-uhr

Balthasar: bal-TAZ-uhr

Baltassar: bal-TAZ-uhr

Bamah: BAY-muh

Bamoth: BAY-mahth

Bamoth Baal: BAY-mahth-**BAY**-uhl or BAY-mahth-buh-**AHL**

Bamoth-baal: BAY-mahth-**BAY**-uhl or BAY-mahth-buh-**AHL**

Bamothbaal: BAY-mahth-BAY-uhl or BAY-mahth-buh-AHL

Ban: ban

Bana: BAY-nuh

Banaa: BAN-ee-uh

Banaia: buh-NYE-uh

Banaias: buh-NYE-uhs

Bane: BAN-ee

Bani: BAY-nye

Banli: BAN-lye

Bannaia: buh-NAY-uh

Bannas: BAN-uhs

Bannus: BAN-uhs

Banuas: BAN-yoo-uhs

Baptist: BAP-tist

Baptizer: BAP-tye-zuhr

Bara: BAY-ruh

Barabbas: buh-RAB-uhs

Barac: BAIR-ak

Barach: BEER-ak

Barachel: BAIR-uh-kuhl

Barachia: BAIR-uh-**KYE**-uh

Barachiah: BAIR-uh-**KYE**-uh

Barachias: BAIR-uh-**KYE**-uhs

Barah: BAIR-uh

Baraia: buh-RYE-uh

Barak: BAIR-ak

Barakel: BAIR-uh-kuhl

Barasa: BAIR-uh-suh

barbarian: bahr-BAIR-ee-uhn

Bared: BEER-ed

Barhumite: bahr-HEW-mite

Baria: buh-RYE-uh

Bariah: buh-RYE-uh

Bar-jesus: bahr-JEE-zuhs

Bar-jona: bahr-JOH-nuh

Barjona: bahr-JOH-nuh

Bar-jonah: bahr-JOH-nuh

Barkos: BAHR-kahs

Barnabas: BAHR-nuh-buhs

Barnea: BAHR-nee-uh

Barodis: buh-ROH-dis

Barsabas: BAHR-suh-buhs

Barsabbas: bahr-SAB-uhs

Barsaith: beer-ZAY-ith

Bartacus: BAHR-tuh-kuhs

Bartholomew: bahr-THAHL-uh-mew

Bartimaeus: BAHR-tuh-**MEE**-uhs

Bartimeus: BAHR-tuh-**MEE**-uhs

Baruch: BAIR-uck

Barzillai: bahr-ZIL-eye

Basaia: BAY-uh-**SEE**-uh

Basaloth: BAS-uh-loth

Basan: BAY-suhn

Bascama: BAS-kuh-muh

Bascath: BAHZ-kahth

Basemath: BAS-uh-math

Bashan: BAY-shuhn

Bashan-havoth-jair: BAY-shuhn-HAY-vahth-**JAY**-uhr

Bashemath: BASH-uh-math

Baskama: BAS-kuh-muh

Basmath: BAS-math

Bason: BAY-suhn

Bastai: BAS-tye

bate: bat

Bat-gader: bat-GAY-duhr

Bath: bath

Bath Rabbim: bath-RAB-im

Bath-rabbim: bath-RAB-im

Bathrabbim: bath-RAB-im

Bath-sheba: bath-SHEE-buh

Bathsheba: bath-SHEE-buh

Bath-shua: bath-SHOO-uh

Bathshua: bath-SHOO-uh

Bathuel: bath-YOO-uhl

Bathzacharias: bath-ZAK-uh-**RYE**-uhs

Bauramite: BAW-ruhm-ite

Bavai: BAY-vye

Bavvai: BAV-eye

Baz: baz

Baziothia: BAZ-ee-oh-**THYE**-uh

Bazlith: BAZ-lith

Bazluth: BAZ-luhth

bdellium. DEL-ee-um

Bealiah: BEE-uh-**LYE**-uh

Bealoth: BEE-uh-loth

Bean: BEE-an

Bebai: BEE-bye

Becher: BEE-kuhr

Becherite: BEE-kuh-rite

Bechor: BEE-kuhr

Bechorath: beh-KOR-ath

Bectileth: BEK-tuh-leth

Bedad: BEE-dad

Bedan: BEE-dan

Bedeiah: beh-DEE-yah

Beeliada: BEE-uh-**LYE**-uh-duh

Beelmeon: BEE-el-**ME**-uhn

Beelphegor: BEE-el-**FEE**-gor

Beelsarus: bee-EL-suh-ruhs

Beelsephon: BEE-uhl-**ZEE**-fun

Beeltethmus: BEE-uhl-**TETH**-muhs

Beelzebub: bee-EL-zeh-buhb

Beelzebul: bee-EL-zeh-buhl

Beer: BEE-uhr

Beera: BEE-uh-ruh

Beerah: BEE-uh-ruh

Beer Elim: BEE-uhr-**EE**-lim

Beer-elim: BEE-uhr-**EE**-lim

Beerelim: BEE-uhr-**EE**-lim

Beeri: BEE-uhr-eye

Beer Lahai Roi: BEE-uhr-luh-**HYE**-roi

Beer-lahai-roi: BEE-uhr-luh-**HYE**-roi

Beerlahairoi: BEE-uhr-luh-**HYE**-roi

Beeroth: BEE-uh-roth

Beeroth Bene-Jaakan: BEE-uh-roth-BEN-eh-**JAY**-uh-kuhn

Beerothite: BEE-uh-ruth-thite

Beer-sheba: BEE-uhr-**SHEE**-buh

Beersheba: BEE-uhr-**SHEE**-buh

Be Eshterah: bee-ESH-tuh-ruh

Be-eshterah: bee-ESH-tuh-ruh

Beesh-terah: bee-ESH-tuh-ruh

Beeshterah: bee-ESH-tuh-ruh

Behemoth: beh-HEE-muhth

beka: BEE-kuh

bekah: BEE-kuh

Beker: BEE-kuhr

Bekerite: BEE-kuhr-ite

Bel: bel

Bela: BEE-luh

Belah: BEE-luh

Belaite: BEE-lay-ite

Belemus: BEL-uh-muhs

Belial: BEE-lee-uhl

Belmaim: bel-MAY-im

Belmain: BEL-mayn

Belmen: BEL-muhn

Belnuus: BEL-noo-uhs

Belshazzar: bel-SHAZ-uhr

Belteshazzar: BEL-tuh-**SHAZ**-er

Beltethmus: bel-TETH-muhs

Bemidbar: buh-MID-bahr

Ben: ben

Ben-abinadab: BEN-uh-**BIN**-uh-dab

Benabinadab: BEN-uh-**BIN**-uh-dab

Benaiah: beh-NAY-uh

Ben-ammi: ben-AM-eye

Benammi: ben-AM-eye

Bendecar: ben-DEE-kuhr

Ben-deker: ben-DEE-kuhr

Bendeker: ben-DEE-kuhr

Bene: BEN-ee

Bene Berak: BEN-ee-**BEER**-ak

Bene-berak: BEN-ee-**BEER**-ak

Beneberak: BEN-ee-**BEER**-ak

Benejaacan: BEN-ee-**JAY**-uh-kuhn

Bene Jaakan: BEN-ee-**JAY**-uh-kuhn

Bene-jaakan: BEN-ee-**JAY**-uh-kuhn

Benejaakan: BEN-ee-**JAY**-uh-kuhn

Bene Jashen: BEN-ee-JAY-shuhn

Bengaber: ben-GEE-buhr

Ben-geber: ben-GEE-buhr

Bengeber: ben-GEE-buhr

Bengui: BEN-gew-eye

Ben-hadad: ben-HAY-dad

Benhadad: ben-HAY-dad

Ben-hail: ben-HAY-uhl

Benhail: ben-HAY-uhl

Ben-hanan: ben-HAY-nuhn

Benhanan: ben-HAY-nuhn

Ben-hesed: ben-HEE-sed

Benhesed: ben-HEE-sed

Ben Hinnom: ben-HIN-uhm

Ben-hinnom: ben-HIN-uhm

Ben-hur: ben-HUHR

Benhur: ben-HUHR

Beninu: bi-NYE-new

Ben-jahaziel: BEN-juh-**HAY**-zee-uhl

Benjamin: BEN-juh-muhn

Benjaminite: BEN-juh-muh-nite

Benjamite: BEN-juh-mite

Ben-josiphiah: BEN-jahs-uh-**FYE**-uh

Beno: BEE-noh

Benob: BEE-nob

Ben-oni: ben-OH-nye

Benoni: ben-OH-nye

Benoth: BEE-nahth

Ben-zoheth: ben-ZOH-heth

Benzoheth: ben-ZOH-heth

Beon: BEE-on

Beor: BEE-or

Bera: BEER-uh

Beracah: BAIR-uh-cuh

Beracha: BAIR-uh-cuh

Berachah: BAIR-uh-cuh

Berachiah: BAIR-uh-**KYE**-uh

Beraiah: beh-RAY-uh

Berakiah: BAIR-uh-**KYE**-uh

Berea: beh-REE-uh

Berean: beh-REE-uhn

Berechiah: BAIR-uh-**KYE**-uh

Bered: BEER-ed

Berekiah: BAIR-uh-**KYE**-uh

Berenice: buhr-uh-**NEES**

Bereshith: BAIR-uh-shith

Beri: BEER-eye

Beria: beh-RYE-uh

Beriah: beh-RYE-uh

Beriahite: beh-**RYE**-uh-HITE

Beriite: beh-RYE-ite

Berite: BEER-ite

Berith: beh-RITH

Bernice: buhr-NEES

Berodach: buh-ROH-dak

Berodach-baladan: buh-ROH-dak-**BAL**-uh-duhn

Beroea: beh-REE-uh

Beroean: beh-REE-uhn

Beromi: beh-ROH-mye

Beroth: BEER-oth

Berotha: beh-ROH-thuh

Berothah: beh-ROH-thuh

Berothai: beh-ROH-thye

Berothite: BEER-uh-thite

Bersabee: beer-SHEE-buh

Berzellai: bar-ZILL-eye

Berzelus: buhr-ZEE-luhs

Besai: BEE-sye

Bescaspasmys: BES-kuhs-**PAZ**-muhs

Besecath: BUHZ-kath

Beseth: BEE-seth

Besodeiah: BES-uh-**DEE**-uh

Besom: BEE-suhm

Besor: BEE-sor

Bessur: BES-uhr

Betah: BEE-tuh

Betane: BET-uh-nee

Bete: BEE-tuh

Beten: BEE-tuhn

Beth: beth

Bethabara: beth-AB-uh-ruh

Beth Acacia: BETH-uh-**KAY**-shuh

Bethacarem: beth-HAK-uh-ruhm

Beth-achzib: beth-AK-zib

Bethanan: beth-HAY-nuhn

Beth Anath: beth-AY-nath

Beth-anath: beth-AY-nath

Bethanath: beth AY-nath

Beth Anoth: beth-AY-noth

Beth-anoth: beth-AY-noth

Bethanoth: beth-AY-noth

Bethany: BETH-uh-nee

Beth Aphrah: beth-AF-ruh

Beth Araba: beth-AIR-uh-buh

Beth-araba: beth-AIR-uh-buh

Betharaba: beth-AIR-uh-buh

Beth-aram: beth-AIR-uhm

Betharan: beth-AY-ruhn

Beth Arbel: beth-AHR-buhl

Beth-arbel: beth-AHR-buhl

Betharbel: beth-AHR-buhl

Beth Ashbea: beth-ASH-bee-uh

Beth-ashbea: beth-ASH-bee-uh

Bethashbea: beth-ASH-bee-uh

Beth-asmoth: beth-AS-moth

Bethasmoth: beth-AS-moth

Beth-astharoth: beth-AS-thuh-rahth

Beth Aven: beth-AY-vuhn

Beth-aven: beth-AY-vuhn

Bethaven: beth-AY-vuhn

Beth Azmaveth: beth-AZ-muh-veth

Beth-azmaveth: beth-AZ-muh-veth

Bethazmaveth: beth-AZ-muh-veth

Beth Baal Meon: beth-BAY-uhl-**MEE**-on

Beth-baal-meon: beth-BAY-uhl-**MEE**-on

Bethbaalmeon: beth-BAY-uhl-**MEE**-on

Beth Barah: beth-BAIR-uh

Beth-barah: beth-BAIR-uh

Bethbarah: beth-BAIR-uh

Beth-basi: beth-BAY-sye

Bethbasi: beth-BAY-sye

Bethbera: beth-BAIR-uh

Bethberai: beth-BEER-ee-eye

Bethbessen: beth-BEE-sehn

Beth-birei: beth-BEER-ee-eye

Beth Biri: beth-BEER-eye

Beth-biri: beth-BEER-eye

Bethbiri: beth-BEER-eye

Beth Car: beth-KAHR

Beth-car: beth-KAHR

Bethcar: beth-KAHR

Bethchar: beth-KAHR

Beth Dagon: beth-DAY-gahn

Beth-dagon: beth-DAY-gahn

Bethdagon. beth-DAY-gahn

Beth Diblathaim: BETH-dib-luh-**THAY**-im

Beth-diblathaim: BETH-dib-luh-**THAY**-im

Bethdiblathaim: BETH-dib-luh-**THAY**-im

Beth Eden: beth-EE-duhn

Beth-eden: beth-EE-duhn

Betheden: beth-EE-duhn

Beth Eglaim: beth-EG-lay-im

Beth-eglaim: beth-EG-lay-im

Betheglaim: beth-EG-lay-im

Beth Eked: beth-EE-kid

Beth-eked: beth-EE-kid

Betheked: beth-EE-kid

Beth-eked-haroim: beth-EE-kid-hah-**ROH**-im

Beth-el: BETH-uhl

Bethel: BETH-uhl

Beth-elite: BETH-uh-lite

Bethelite: BETH-uh-lite

Bethelsarezer: BETH-uhl-suh-**REE**-zuhr

Bethemec: beth-EE-mehk

Beth Emek: beth-EE-mehk

Beth-emek: beth-EE-mehk

Bethemek: beth-EE-mehk

Bether: BEE-thuhr

Bethesda: buh-THEZ-duh

Beth Ezel: beth-EE-zuhl

Beth-ezel: beth-EE-zuhl

Bethezel: beth-EE-zuhl

Beth Gadar: beth-GAY-duhr

Beth Gader: beth-GAY-duhr

Beth-gader: beth-GAY-duhr

Bethgader: beth-GAY-duhr

Beth Gamul: beth-GAY-muhl

Beth-gamul: beth-GAY-muhl

Bethgamul: beth-GAY-muhl

Beth Gilgal: beth-GIL-gal

Beth-gilgal: beth-GIL-gal

Bethgilgal: beth-GIL-gal

Beth Haccerem: beth-HAK-uh-rem

Beth-haccerem: beth-HAK-uh-rem

Beth Haccherem: beth-HAK-uh-rem

Beth-haccherem: beth-HAK-uh-rem

Bethhaccherem: beth-HAK-uh-rem

Beth-ha-Cherem: beth-HAK-uh-rem

Beth Haggan: beth-HAG-uhn

Beth-haggan: beth-HAG-uhn

Bethhaggan: beth-HAG-uhn

Beth-Hagla: beth-HAG-luh

Beth Hakkerem: beth-HAK-uh-rem

Beth-hanan: beth-HAY-nuhn

Beth Haram: beth-HAIR-uhm

Beth-haram: beth-HAIR-uhm

Bethharam: beth-HAIR-uhm

Beth Haran: beth-HAIR-uhn

Beth-haran: beth-HAIR-uhn

Bethharan: beth-HAIR-uhn

Beth-hogla: beth-HOG-luh

Beth Hoglah: beth-HOG-luh

Beth-hoglah: beth-HOG-luh

Bethhoglah: beth-HOG-luh

Beth Horon: beth-HOR-uhn

Beth-horon: beth-HOR-uhn

Bethhoron: beth-HOR-uhn

Bethia: beh-THEE-uh

Bethiesimoth: beth-JESH-eh-mahth

Beth Jeshimoth: beth-JESH-eh-mahth

Beth-jeshimoth: beth-JESH-eh-mahth

Bethjeshimoth: beth-JESH-eh-mahth

Beth Jesimoth: beth-JES-eh-mahth

Beth-jesimoth: beth-JES-eh-mahth

Beth-leaphrah: BETH-leh-**AF**-ruh

Beth-le-aphrah: BETH-leh-**AF**-ruh

Bethleaphrah: BETH-leh-**AF**-ruh

Beth Lebaoth: BETH-leh-**BAY**-oth

Beth-lebaoth: BETH-leh-**BAY**-oth

Bethlebaoth: BETH-leh-**BAY**-oth

Beth-lehem: BETH-leh-hem

Bethlehem: BETH-leh-hem

Beth-lehem Ephratah: BETH-leh-hem-**EF**-ruh-tuh

Beth-lehem Ephrathah: BETH-leh-hem-**EF**-ruh-thuh

Bethlehem Ephratah: BETH-leh-hem-**EF**-ruh-tuh

Bethlehem-ephrathah: BETH-leh-hem-**EF**-ruh-thuh

Beth-lehemite: BETH-leh-hem-ite

Bethlehemite: BETH-leh-hem-ite

Beth-lehem-judah: BETH-leh-hem-**JOO**-duh

Beth-lomon: beth-LOH-muhn

Beth-maacah: beth-MAY-uh-cuh

Bethmaacah: beth-MAY-uh-cuh

Beth Maachah: beth-MAY-uh-cuh

Beth-maachah: beth-MAY-uh-cuh

Bethmaacha: beth-MAY-uh-cuh

Bethmaon: beth-MAY-on

Beth Marcaboth: beth-MAHR-kuh-bahth

Beth-marcaboth: beth-MAHR-kuh-bahth

Bethmarcaboth: beth-MAHR-kuh-bahth

Bethmarchaboth: beth-MAHR-kuh-bahth

Beth Meon: beth-MEE-on

Beth-meon: beth-MEE-on

Bethmeon: beth-MEE-on

Beth Millo: beth-MIL-oh

Beth-millo: beth-MIL-oh

Bethmillo: beth-MIL-oh

Bethnemra: Beth NIM-rah

Beth Nimrah: beth-NIM-ruh

Beth-nimrah: beth-NIM-ruh

Bethnimrah: beth-NIM-ruh

Beth Ophrah: beth-AHF-ruh

Beth-ophrah: beth-AHF-ruh

Beth-oron: beth-OR-uhn

Beth-palet: beth-PAY-let

Beth Pazzez: beth-PAZ-iz

Beth-pazzez: beth-PAZ-iz

Bethpazzez: beth-PAZ-iz

Beth Pelet: beth-PEE-lit

Beth-pelet: beth-PEE-lit

Bethpelet: beth-PEE-lit

Beth Peor: beth-PEE-or

Beth-peor: beth-PEE-or

Bethpeor: beth-PEE-or

Bethphage: BETH-fuh-jee

Beth-phelet: beth-FEE-lit

Bethphelet: beth-FEE-lit

Bethpheses: beth-PAZ-iz

Bethphogor: beth-FOH-gohr

Beth Rapha: beth-RAY-fuh

Beth-rapha: beth-RAY-fuh

Bethrapha: beth-RAY-fuh

Beth Rechab: beth-REE-kab

Beth Rehob: beth-REE-hahb

Beth-rehob: beth-REE-hahb

Bethrehob: beth-REE-hahb

Bethsabee: beth-SAY-buh-ee

Beth-saida: beth-SAY-uh-duh

Bethsaida: beth-SAY-uh-duh

Bethsames: beth-SAM-ehs

Bethsamos: beth-SAM-ahs

Bethsan: beth-SAN

Bethsetta: beth-SET-uh

Beth Shan: beth-SHAN

Beth-shan: beth-SHAN

Bethshan: beth-SHAN

Beth Shean: beth-SHEE-uhn

Beth-shean: beth-SHEE-uhn

Bethshean: beth-SHEE-uhn

Beth Shemesh: beth-SHEH-mish

Beth-shemesh: beth-SHEH-mish

Bethshemesh: beth-SHEH-mish

Beth-shemite: beth-SHEM-ite

Bethshemite: beth-SHEM-ite

Beth Shittah: beth-SHIT-uh

Beth-shittah: beth-SHIT-uh

Bethshittah: beth-SHIT-uh

Bethsi: beth-SYE

Bethsimoth: beth-SYE-mahth

Bethsur: beth-SOOR

Bethsura: beth-SOOR-uh

Beth Tappuah: beth-TAP-yoo-uh

Beth-tappuah: beth-TAP-yoo-uh

Bethtappuah: beth-TAP-yoo-uh

Beththaphua: beth-TAP-yoo-uh

Beth Togarmah: BETH-toh-**GAHR**-muh

Beth-togarmah: BETH-toh-**GAHR**-muh

Bethtogarmah: BETH-toh-**GAHR**-muh

Bethuel: beth-YEW-uhl

Bethul: BETH-uhl

Bethulia: beth-YEW-lee-uh

Bethzacharam: beth-ZAK-uh-ram

Beth-zaith: beth-ZAY-ith

Bethzatha: beth-ZAY-thuh

Beth-zatha: beth-ZAY-thuh

Bethzecha: beth-ZEE-kuh

Beth-zechariah: beth-ZEK-uh-**RYE**-uh

Beth Zur: beth-ZUHR

Beth-zur: beth-ZUHR

Bethzur: beth-ZUHR

Betolius: beh-TOH-lee-uhs

Betomasthaim: BET-uh-mas-**THAY**-im

Betomastham: BET-uh-**MAS**-thuhm

Betomesthaim: BET-uh-mis-**THAY**-im

Betomestham: BET-uh-**MES**-thuhm

Betonim: BET-uh-nim

Beulah: BEW-luh

Bezaanannim: beh-ZAY-uh-**NAN**-im

Bezai: BEE-zye

Bezaleel: beh-ZAL-ee-uhl

Bezalel: BEZ-uh-lel

Bezec: BEE-zek

Bezek: BEE-zek

Bezeleel: BEZ-eh-**LEE**-uhl

Bezer: BEE-zuhr

Bezeth: BEE-zeth

Bezetha: BEE-zuh-thuh

Biatas: BYE-uh-tuhs

Bichri: BIK-rye

Bichrite: BIK-rite

Bicri: BIK-rye

Bidkar: BID-kahr

Bigtha: BIG-thuh

Bigthan: BIG-thuhn

Bigthana: BIG-thuh-nuh

Bigvai: BIG-vye

Bikri: BIK-rye

Bildad: BIL-dad

Bileam: BIL-ee-uhm

Bilgah: BIL-guh

Bilgai: BIL-gye

Bilhah: BILL-hah

Bilhan: BIL-han

Bilshan: BIL-shan

Bimhal: BIM-hal

Binea: BIN-ee-uh

Binnui: BIN-yoo-eye

Birei: BEER-ee-eye

Biri: BEER-eye

Birsha: BEER-shuh

Birzaith: beer-ZAY-ith

Birzavith: beer-ZAY-vith

Bishlam: BISH-luhm

Bithia: BITH-ee-uh

Bithiah: beh-**THYE**-uh

Bithron: BITH-rahn

Bithynia: beh-THIN-ee-uh

Biziothiah: BIZ-ee-oh-**THYE**-uh

Bizjothjah: biz-JAHTH-juh

Biztha: BIZ-thuh

Blastus: BLAS-tuhs

Boanerges: BOH-uh-**NUHR**-jeez

Boaz: BOH-az

Boccas: BAH-kuhs

Bocci: BAHK-eye

Bocheru: BAHK-eh-roo

Bochim: BOH-kim

Bochri: BAHK-rye

Bochru: BAHK-roo

Boen: BOH-ehn

Bohan: BOH-han

Bokeru: BOH-kuh-roo

Bokim: BOH-kim

Boni: BOH-nye

Bonni: BOH-nye

Booz: BOH-ahz

Bor Ashan: bor-AY-shuhn

Bor-ashan: bor-AY-shuhn

Borashan: bor-AY-shuhn

Borith: BOR-ith

Boscath: BAHS-kath

Bosketh: BAHS-kehth

Boses: BOH-zez

Bosor: BOH-sor

Bosora: BAHS-uh-ruh

Bosphorus: BAHS-fuh-ruhs

Bosra: BAHZ-ruh

Bougaean: boo-GEE-uhn

Bozez: BOH-ziz

Bozkath: BAHZ-kath

Boznai: BAHZ-nye

Bozrah: BAHZ-ruh

Brie: buhr-EYE-uh

bruchus: BRUH-kuhs

bubale: boo-BAYL

Bubastis: bew-BAS-tis

Bubastus: bew-BAS-tuhs

Bukki: BUHK-eye

Bukkiah: buh-KYE-uh

Bul: bool

Buna: BEW-nuh

Bunah: BEW-nuh

Bunni: BUHN-eye

Buz: buhz

Buzi: BEW-zye

Buzite: BEW-zite

Byblos: BIB-lahs

C

Caanan: KAY-uh-nuhn

Caath: KAY-ath

Caathite: KAY-uh-thite

cab: kab

Cabbon: KAB-uhn

Cabseel: KAB-zee-el

Cabul: KAY-buhl

Cad: kad

Caddis: KAD-is

Cademoth: KID-eh-muhth

Cades: KAY-deez

Cades-barne: KAY-deez-**BAHR**-nee

Cadesbarne: KAY-deez-**BAHR**-nee

Cadmiel: KAD-mee-uhl

Caesar: SEE-zuhr

Caesaraea: SES-uh-**REE**-uh

Caesaraea-Philippi: SES-uh-REE-uh-**FIL**-eh-pye or SES-uh-REE-uh-fil-**IP**-eye

Caesarea: SES-uh-**REE**-uh

Caesarea-Philippi: SES-uh-REE-uh-**FIL**-eh-pye or SES-uh-REE-uh-fil-**IP**-eye

Cadumim: KAY-duh-mim

Caiaphas: KYE-uh-fuhs or KAY-uh-fuhs

Cain: kayn

Cainan: KAY-nuhn

Calah: KAY-luh

Calamolalus: KAL-uh-**MAHL**-uh-luhs

calamus: KAL-uh-muhs

Calano: KAL-noh

Calcol: KAL-kahl

Caleb: KAY-luhb
Caleb-ephratah: KAY-luhb-**EF**-ruh-tuh
Caleb Ephrathah: KAY-luhb-**EF**-ruh-thuh
Caleb-ephrathah: KAY-luhb-**EF**-ruh-thuh
Calebite: KAY-luhb-ite
Calitas: kuh-LYE-tuhs
Callisthenes: kuh-LISS-thuh-neez
Calneh: KAL-nuh
Calno: KAL-noh
Calor: KAY-lor
Calphi: KAL-fye
Calubi: kuh-LOO-bye
Calvary: KAL-vuh-ree
camelopardalus: kuhm-MEL-oh-**PAR**-duh-luhs
Camon: KAY-muhn
camphire: KAM-fyer
Camuel: KIM-yoo-uhl
Cana: KAY-nuh
Canaan: KAY-nuhn
Canaanite: KAY-nuh-nite
Canaanitess: KAY-nuh-nite-es
Canaanitish: KAY-nuh-nite-ish
Cananaean: KAY-nuh-**NEE**-uhn
Canath: KEE-nath
Candace: KAN-duh-see
Canneh: KAN-uh
Canticle: KAN-ti-kuhl
Capernaum: kuh-PUHR-nay-uhm
Cape-salmone: KAYP-sal-**MOH**-nee
caph: kahf
Caphara: keh-FAH-ruh
Capharnaum: kuh-FAHR-nay-uhm
Caphar-salama: KAF-uhr-**SAL**-uh-muh
Capharsalama: KAF-uhr-**SAL**-uh-muh
Caphenatha: kuh-FEN-uh-thuh

Caphetetha: kuh-FET-uh-thuh

Caphira: kuh-FYE-ruh

Caphirim: kuh-FYE-rim

Caphthorim: KAF-thuh-rim

Caphtor: KAF-tor

Caphtorim: KAF-tuh-rim

Caphtorite: KAF-tuh-rite

Cappadocia: KAP-uh-**DOH**-shee-uh

Car: kahr

Carabasion: KAIR-uh-**BAY**-zhee-uhn

Carcaa: kahr-KAY-uh

Carcas: KAHR-kuhs

Carchamis: KAHR-kuh-mis

Carchemish: KAHR-kuh-mish

Careah: kuh-REE-uh

Caree: kuh-REE-uh

Carehim: KOR-uh-him

Carem: KAIR-uhm

Caria: KAIR-ee-uh

Carian: KAIR-ee-uhn

Cariath-Arbe: KAIR-ee-ahth-**AHR**-buh

Cariathbaal: KAIR-ee-ahth-**BAY**-uhl or KEER-ee-ahth-bah-**AHL**

Cariathaim: KAIR-ee-ahth-**AY**-im

Cariathiarim: KAIR-ee-ahth-**EYE**-uh-rim

Cariath-senna: KAIR-ee-ahth-**SEN**-uh

Cariath-Sepher: KAIR-ee-ahth-**SEE**-fuhr

Carioth: KAIR-ee-ahth

Carite: KAIR-ite

Carith: KAIR-ith

Carkas: KAHR-kuhs

Carmanian: kahr-MAY-nee-uhn

Carme: KAHR-mee

Carmel: KAHR-muhl

Carmelite: KAHR-muh-lite

Carmelitess: KAHR-muh-lite-es

Carmi: KAHR-mye

Carmite: KAHR-mite

Carmonian: kahr-MOH-nee-uhn

Carnaim: kahr-NAY-im

Carnion: KAHR-nee-uhn

Carpus: KAHR-puhs

Carshena: kahr-SHEE-nuh

Cartha: KAHR-tuh

Carthaginian: KAHR-thuh-**JIN**-ee-uhn

Carthan: KAHR-than

Casaia: kuh-SYE-uh

Casaloth: kah-SAHL-uth

Casbon: KAS-bahn

Casiphia: kuh-SIF-ee-uh

Casleu: KAS-loo

Casluh: KAS-luh

Casluhim: KAS-luh-him

Casluhite: KAS-luh-hite

Casluim: KAS-luh-him

Casphin: KAS-fin

Casphor: KAS-for

Caspin: KAS-pin

Cassia: kaz-ZYE-uh

cassia: KASH-uh

Castor: KAS-tuhr

Cater: KAT-uhr

Cateth: KAT-ath

Cathua: kuh-THOO-uh

Cauda: KAW-duh

Cedar: KEE-duhr

cedar: SEE-duhr

Cedemite: KED-uh-mite

Cedes: KEE-des

Cedma: KED-muh

Cedron: KID-ruhn or SEE-druhn

Ceelatha: KEE-uh-**LAY**-thuh

Ceila: kah-EYE-luh

Ceilan: SEE-luhn

Celesyria: SEL-uh-**SEER**-ee-uh or SEE-luh-**SEER**-ee-uh

Celosyria: SEL-oh-**SEER**-ee-uh or SEE-loh-**SIHR**-ee-uh

Cenchrea: SEN-kree-uh

Cenchreae: SEN-kruh-ee

Cendebaeus: SEN-duh-**BEE**-uhs

Cendebeus: SEN-duh-**BEE**-uhs

Cenereth: KIN-uhr-eth

Ceneroth: KIN-uhr-ahth

Cenez: KEE-naz

Cenezite: KEN-uh-zite

Ceni: KEN-eye

Cenneroth: KIN-uhr-ahth

Cephas: SEE-fuhs

Cera: KEER-uh

Cerethi: KAIR-uh-thye

Cesar: SEE-zuhr

Cesarea: SES-uh-**REE**-uh

Ceseleththabor: KES-leth-**TAY**-bohr

Cesil: KEE-suhl

Cesion: KISH-ee-ahn

Cetab: SEE-tab

Cetean: seh-TEE-uhn

Cethim: KIT-tim

Cethite: KIT-ite

Cethlis: KITH-lis

Cetron: KIT-run

Cetura: kah-TEW-ruh

Chabod: kah-BOHD

Chabris: KAB-ris

Chabul: KAY-buhl

Chadias: KAY-dee-uhs

Chadiasan: KAY-dee-**AY**-shuhn

Chaereas: KEER-ee-uhs

Chalanne: KAL-uh-nuh

chalcedony: kal-SED-uh-nee

Chalchal: KAL-kahl

Chalcol: KAL-kohl

Chaldaea: kal-DEE-uh

Chaldaean: kal-DEE-uhn

Chaldea: kal-DEE-uh

Chaldean: kal-DEE-uhn

Chaldee: kal-DEE

Chaldees: kal-DEEZ

Chale: KAY-luh

Chali: KAY-lye

Chalane: KAL-nuh

Chalphi: KAL-fye

Cham: kam

Chamaal: KIM-al

Chamaam: KIM-ham

Chamath: KAM-eth

Chamos: KAM-ahs

Chanaan: KAY-nuhn

Chanaana: kuh-NAY-uh-nuh

Chanana: kuh-NAY-nuh

Channuneus: KAN-uh-**NEE**-uhs

Chaphenatha: kuh-FEN-uh-thuh

Charaathalar: KAIR-ay-**ATH**-uh-lahr

Characa: KAIR-uh-kuh

charadrion: kair-AD-ree-ahn

Charan: KEE-ruhn

Charashim: KAIR-uh-shim

Charax: KAIR-aks

Charchamis: KAHR-kuh-mis

Charchemish: KAHR-kuh-mish

Charcus: KAHR-kuhs

Charea: KAIR-ee-uh

charmel: KAHR-mel

Charmi: KAHR-mye

Charmis: KAHR-mis

Charran: KAIR-uhn

Chaseba: KAS-uh-buh

Chaselon: KISS-luhn

Chaspho: KAS-foh

Chebar: KEE-bahr

Chebbon: KAB-uhn

Chebron: KEE-bruhn

Chedor-Laomer: KEH-duhr-lay-**OH**-muhr

Chedorlaomer: KEH-duhr-lay-**OH**-muhr

Chelal: KEE-lal

Chelcias: KEL-shee-uhs

Cheleab: KEL-ee-ab

Cheleoud: KEL-ee-ood

Chelion: KEL-ee-uhn

Chellean: KEL-ee-uhn

Chellian: KEL-ee-uhn

Chelluh: KEL-uh

Chellus: KEL-uhs

Chelmad: KEL-mad

Chelod: KEE-lahd

Chelous: KEL-uhs

Chelub: KEE-luhb

Chelubai: ki-LOO-bye

Cheluh: KEL-uh

Cheluhi: KEL-uh-hye

Chemarim: KEM-uh-rim

Chemosh: KEE-mosh

Chenaanah: ki-NAY-uh-nuh

Chenani: ki-NAY-nye

Chenaniah: KEN-uh-**NYE**-uh

Chene: KAN-uh

Chephar-ammoni: KEE-fuhr-**AM**-uh-nye

Chepharammoni: KEE-fuhr-**AM**-uh-nye

Chephar Haammoni: KEE-fuhr-hay-**AM**-uh-nye

Chephar-haammoni: KEE-fuhr-hay-**AM**-uh-nye

Chephirah: ki-FYE-ruh

Chephirim: KEF-uh-rim

Cheran: KEER-uhn

Chereas: KEER-ee-uhs

Cherethim: KER-uh-thim

Cherethite: KER-uh-thite

Cherith: KER-ith

cherogril: KAIR-oh-gril

Cherub: KER-uhb

cherub: CHAIR-uhb

cherubim: CHAIR-uh-bim

Chesalon: KES-uh-lon

Chesed: KEE-sed

Chesil: KEE-suhl

Cheslon: KES-lon

Chesulloth: ki-SUHL-oth

cheth: keth

Chettiim: KET-uh-im

Chezib: KEE-zib

Chidon: KYE-duhn

Chileab: KIL-ee-ab

Chilion: KIL-ee-uhn

Chilmad: KIL-mad

Chimham: KIM-ham

Chinnereth: KIN-uh-reth

Chinneroth: KIN-uh-roth

Chios: KYE-ahs

Chisleu: KIZ-loo

Chislev: KIZ-lev

Chislon: KIZ-lon

Chisloth Tabor: KIZ-loth-**TAY**-buhr

Chisloth-tabor: KIZ-loth-**TAY**-buhr

Chislothtabor: KIZ-loth-**TAY**-buhr

Chitlish: KIT-lish

Chittim: KIT-im

Chiun: KYE-uhn

Chloe: KLOH-ee

Choba: KOH-buh

Chobar: KOH-bar

chodchod. KOHD-kohd

Chodorlahomor: KOH-duh-lay-**OH**-mahr

Chonenias: KEN-uh-**NYE**-uhs

Chor-ashan: kor-AY-shuhn

Chorashan: kor-AY-shuhn

Chorazin: koh-RAY-zin

Chorbe: KOR-bee

Chosamaeus: KAHS-uh-**MEE**-uhs

Chozeba: koh-ZEE-buh

Christ: kryst

Christian: KRIS-chuhn

Chronicle: KRON-eh-kuhl

chrysolite: KRIS-uh-lite

chrysoprase: KRIS-uh-prayz

chrysoprasus: KRIS-uh-**PRAY**-zuhs

Chub: kuhb

Chun: kuhn

Chus: koosh

Chusai: KEW-shy

Chusan Rasathaim: KEW-shan-RAHSH-uh-**THAY**-im

Chusham: KEW-sham

Chushan-rishathaim: KEW-shan-RISH-uh-**THAY**-im

Chusi: KEW-shy

Chuza: KEW-zuh

Cibsaim: kib-ZAY-im

Cidimoth: KID-uh-moth

Cilicia: suh-LISH-ee-uh

Cin: kayn

Cina: KYN-uh

Cinite: KEN-ite

Cinneroth: SIN-uh-roth

Cirama: suh-RAY-muh

Cis: sis

Cisai: SYE-sye

Cison: KYE-sahn

Cisson: KYE-sahn

Cithara: SITH-uh-ruh

Cithern: SITH-uhrn

Citim: SIT-im

Clauda: KLAW-duh

Claudia: KLAW-dee-uh

Claudius: KLAW-dee-uhs

Clement: KLEM-uhnt

Cleopas: KLEE-oh-puhs

Cleopatra: KLEE-oh-**PAT**-ruh

Cleophas: KLEE-oh-fuhs

Coa: KOH-uh

Colias: koh-LAY-uhs

Clopas: KLOH-puhs

Cnidus: NYE-duhs

Coele-syria: SEE-lee-**SEER**-ee-uh

Coelesyria: SEE-lee-**SEER**-ee-uh

Col: kahl

Col-hozeh: kol-HOH-zuh

Colhozeh: kol-HOH-zuh

Colius: koh-LYE-uhs

Colossae: kuh-LOS-ee

Colosse: kuh-LOS-ee

Colossian: kuh-LOSH-uhn

Comforter: KUHM-for-tuhr

Conaniah: KON-uh-**NYE**-uh

Coniah: koh-NYE-uh

Cononiah: KON-uh-**NYE**-uh

Coos: KOH-ahs

Coph: kohf

Cor: kor

Corashan: kor-ASH-uhn

Corban: KOR-ban

Corbe: KOR-bee

Core: KOH-ruh or KOH-ree

Corinth: KOR-inth

Corinthian: kuh-RIN-thee-uhn

Corinthus: kuh-RIN-thuhs

Corite: KOR-ite

Cornelius: kor-NEE-lee-uhs or kor-NEEL-yuhs

Cornustibii: KOHR-nuhs-**TIB**-ee-eye

Corozain: koh-RAY-zin

Cos: kos

Cosam: KOH-suhm

coulter: KOHL-tuhr

Council: KOUN-suhl

Counseller: KOUN-suh-luhr

Counsellor: KOUN-suh-luhr

Counselor: KOUN-suh-luhr

Coutha: KOO-thuh

Covenant: KUH-vuh-nuhnt

Coz: koz

Cozbi: KOZ-bye

Cozeba: koh-ZEE-buh

Crates: KRAY-teez

Creator: kree-AY-tuhr

Crescens: KRES-uhnz

Cretan: KREE-tuhn

Crete: kreet

Cretian: KREE-shuhn

Crispus: KRIS-puhs

Cub: kuhb

cubit: KEW-bit

Culom: KOO-luhm

Culon: KOO-luhn

cumi: KEW-mee

cumin: KUH-min

cummin: KUH-min

Cun: kuhn

Cush: koosh

Cushan: KOOSH-an

Cushan-rishathaim: KOOSH-an-RISH-uh-**THAY**-im

Cushanrishathaim: KOOSH-an-RISH-uh-**THAY**-im

Cushi: KOOSH-eye

Cushite: KOOSH-ite

Cusi: KOOSH-eye

Cuth: kooth

Cutha: KOOTH-uh

Cuthah: KOOTH-uh

Cuthites: KEW-thites

Cuza: KOO-zuh

Cyamon: SYE-uh-muhn

Cyaxares: sye-AKS-uh-reez

Cyprian: SIP-ree-uhn

Cypriot: SIP-ree-uht

Cyprus: SYE-pruhs

Cyrene: sye-REE-nee

Cyrenean: sye-REE-nee-uhn

Cyreni: sye-REE-nee

Cyrenian: sye-REE-nee-uhn

Cyrenius: sye-REE-nee-uhs

Cyrus: SYE-ruhs

D

Daas: DAY-as

Dabareh: DAB-uh-ruh

Dabbasheth: DAB-uh-sheth

Dabbesheth: DAB-uh-sheth

Daberath: DAB-uh-rath

Dabereth: DAB-uh-reth

Dabir: DAY-buhr

Dabria: DAB-ree-uh

Dacobi: DAY-kuh-bye

Dadan: DAY-duhn

Daddeus: DAD-ee-uhs

Dadu: DAY-doo

Dagon: DAY-gahn

Daisan: DAY-suhn

Dalaia: duh-LAY-uh

Dalaiah: duh-LAY-uh

Dalaias: duh-LAY-uhs

daleth: DAH-leth

Dalila: duh-LYE-luh

Dalmanutha: DAL-muh-**NOO**-thuh

Dalmatia: dal-MAY-shee-uh

Dalphon: DAL-fahn

Damaris: DAM-uh-ris

Damascene: DAM-uh-seen

Damascus: duh-MAS-kuhs

Dammin: DAM-in

Damna: DAM-nuh

Dan: dan

Daniel: DAN-yuhl

Danite: DAN-ite

Dan Jaan: dan-JAY-uhn

Dan-jaan: dan-JAY-uhn

Danna: DAN-uh

Dannah: DAN-uh

Daphca: DAF-cuh

Daphne: DAF-nee

Daphnis: DAF-nis

Dara: DAIR-uh

Darda: DAHR-duh

daric: dair-ik

Darius: duh-RYE-uhs

Darkon: DAHR-kahn

Dathan- DAY-thuhn

Dathema: DATH-uh-muh

Datheman: DATH-eh-muhn

David: DAY-vid

daysman: DAYS-muhn

Day Star: DAY-stahr

Day-star: DAY-stahr

Daystar: DAY-stahr

deacon: DEE-kuhn

deaconess: DEE-kuh-nes

Debar: DEE-buhr

Debara: DEE-buhr-uh

Debarim: DEE-buh-rim

Debbaseth: DEB-uh-seth

Debbora: DEB-uh-ruh

Debelaim: DIB-lay-im

Debir: DEE-buhr

Deblatha: DIB-luh-thuh

Deblathaim: DIB-luh-**THAY**-im

Debora: DEB-uh-ruh

Deborah: DEB-uh-ruh

Decapolis: di-KAP-uh-lis

Decla: DIK-luh

Dedan: DEE-duhn

Dedanim: DEE-duh-nim

Dedanite: DEE-duh-nite

Dehavite: di-HAY-vite

Deity: DEE-uh-tee

Dekar: DEE-kuhr

Deker: DEE-kuhr

Delaiah: deh-LAY-uh

Delean: dye-LEE-uhn

Delilah: deh-LYE-luh

Delos: DEE-lahs

Delus: DEE-luhs

Demas: DEE-muhs

Demetrius: duh-MEE-tree-uhs

demoniac: deh-MOH-nee-ak or deh-MAH-nee-ak

Demophon: DEM-uh-fahn

Denaba: DEN-uh-buh

denarii: deh-NAIR-ee-eye

denarius: deh-NAIR-ee-uhs

Derbe: DUHR-bee

Dessau: DES-aw

Deuel: DOO-uhl

Deuteronomy: DOO-tuh-**RON**-uh-mee

Devil: DEV-uhl

Diana: dye-AN-uh

Diaspora: dye-AS-puh-ruh

Diblah: DIB-luh

Diblaim: DIB-lay-im

Diblath: DIB-lath

Diblathaim: DIB-luh-**THAY**-im

Dibon: DYE-bahn

Dibon Gad: DYE-bahn-**GAD**

Dibon-gad: DYE-bahn-**GAD**

Dibongad: DYE-bahn-**GAD**

Dibri: DIB-rye

didrachmas: deh-DRAK-muhs

Didymus: DID-uh-muhs

Dies: DYE-es

Diklah: DIK-luh

Dilean: DIL-ee-uhn

Dimnah: DIM-nuh

Dimon: DYE-muhn

Dimona: deh-MOH-nah

Dimonah: deh-MOH-nah

Dinah: DYE-nuh

Dinaite: DYE-nay-ite

Dinhabah: DIN-huh-buh

Dionysius: DYE-uh-**NISH**-ee-uhs

Dionysus: DYE-uh-**NYE**-suhs

Dioscorinthius: DYE-uhs-kuh-**RIN**-thee-uhs

Dioscorus: DYE-oh-**SKOHR**-uhs

Diotrephes: dye-AHT-ruh-feez

Diphath: DYE-fath

Disan: DYE-shan

disciple: di-SYE-puhl

Dishan: DYE-shan

Dishon: DYE-shahn

Dison: DYE-sahn

Dizahab: DIZ-uh-hab

Di-zahab: dye-ZAY-hab

Doch: dahk

Docus: DOH-kuhs

Dodai: DOH-dye

Dodanim: DOH-duh-nim

Dodavah: DOH-duh-vuh

Dodavahu: DOH-duh-**VAY**-hew

Dodavhu: doh-DAV-hew

Dodo: DOH-doh

Doeg: DOH-ehg

Dok: dok

Dommim: DAM-im

Donary: DOH-nuh-ree

Dophkah: DAHF-kuh

Dor: dor

Dora: DOR-uh

Dorcas: DOR-kuhs

Dorda: DAR-duh

Dorymenes: dor-IM-uh-neez

Dorymenus: dor-IM-uh-nooz

Dositheus: doh-SITH-ee-uhs

Dothan: DOH-thuhn

drachma: DRAK-muh

Drimylus: DRIM-uh-luhs

Drusilla: droo-SIL-ul

Duel: DOO-uhl

Duma: DOO-muh

Dumah: DOO-muh

Dura: DOO-ruh

E

Eanes: EE-uh-neez

Easter: EE-stuhr

Ebal: EE-buhl

Ebed: EE-bid

Ebed-melech: EE-bid-**MEE**-lick

Ebedmelech: EE-bid-**MEE**-lick

Ebed-Melek: EE-bid-**MEE**-lick

Eben-bohan-ben-reuben: EE-ben-BOH-han-ben-**ROO**-ben

Ebenezer: EB-uh-**NEE**-zuhr

Eber: EE-buhr

Ebez: EE-behz

Ebiasaph: eh-BYE-uh-saf

Ebron: EE-bruhn

Ebronah: eh-BROH-nuh

Ecanus: eh-KAY-nuhs

Ecbatana: ek-BAT-uh-nuh

Ecclesiastes: eh-KLEE-zee-**AS**-teez

Ecclesiasticus: eh-KLEE-zee-**AS**-ti-kuhs

Edar: EE-duhr

Eddias: eh-DYE-uhs

Edema: AD-eh-muh

Eden: EE-duhn

Edenite: EE-duh-nite

Eder : EE-duhr

Edes: EE-deez

Edna: ED-nuh

Ednas: ED-nuhs

Edom: EE-duhm

Edomite: EE-duh-mite

Edrai: ED-ray-eye

Edrei: ED-ree-eye

Edri: ED-rye

Egla: EG-luh

Eglah: EG-luh

Eglaim: EG-lay-im

Eglath Shelishiyah: EG-lath-sheh-**LISH**-uh-yuh

Eglath-shelishiyah: EG-lath-sheh-**LISH**-uh-yuh

Eglathshelishiyah: EG-lath-sheh-**LISH**-uh-yuh

Eglon: EG-lahn

Egrebel: eh-GREE-buhl

Egypt: EE-jipt

Egyptian: eh-JIP-shuhn

Ehi: EE-hye

Ehac: EE-hak

Ehud: EE-huhd

Ekah: EE-kuh

Eker: EE-kuhr

Ekrebel: EK-ruh-buhl

Ekron: EK-ruhn

Ekronite: EK-ruh-nite

EL: el

Ela: EE-luh

Elad: EL-ee-uhd

Elada: EL-uh-duh

Eladah: EL-uh-duh

Elah: EE-luh

Elam: EE-luhm

Elamite: EE-luh-mite

Elasa: EL-uh-suh

Elasah: EL-uh-suh

Elath: EE-lath

El-berith: EL-beh-**RITH**

Elberith: EL-beh-**RITH**

El Bethel: el-BETH-uhl

El-bethel: el-BETH-uhl

El-beth-el: el-BETH-uhl

Elbethel: el-BETH-uhl

Elcana: el-KAY-nuh

Elcesite: EL-kuh-syte

Elchanan: el-KAY-nuhn

Elcia: el-KYE-uh

Eldaa: el-DAY-uh

Eldaah: el-DAY-uh

Eldad: EL-dad

Elead: EL-ee-uhd

Eleadah: EL-ee-**AY**-duh

Eleale: EL-lee-**AY**-lah

Elealeh: EL-lee-**AY**-lah

Eleasa: EL-ee-**AY**-suh

Eleasah: EL-ee-**AY**-suh

Eleazar: EL-ee-**AY**-zuhr

Eleazurus: EL-ee-uh-**ZOOR**-uhs

Elehanan: el-HAY-nuhn

El Elohe Israel: el-EL-oh-heh-IS-ray-uhl

El-elohe-israel: el-EL-oh-heh-IS-ray-uhl

El Elyon: EL-el-yohn

El-elyon: EL-el-yohn

eleph: EE-lif

Eleutherus: eh-LOO-thuh-ruhs

Elhanan: el-HAY-nuhn

Eli: EE-lye

Elia: eh-LYE-uh

Eliab: eh-LYE-uhb

Eliaba: eh-LYE-uh-buh

Eliacim: eh-LYE-uh-kim

Eliada: eh-LYE-uh-duh

Eliadah: eh-LYE-uh-duh

Eliadas: eh-LYE-uh-duhs

Eliadun: eh-LYE-uh-duhn

Eliah: eh-LYE-uh

Eliahba: eh-LYE-uh-buh

Eliakim: eh-LYE-uh-kim

Elial: eh-LYE-uhl

Eliali: eh-LYE-uh-lye

Elialis: eh-LYE-uh-lis

Eliam: uh-LYE-uhm

Eliaonlas: eh-LYE-uh-**NYE**-uhs

Elias: eh-LYE-uhs

Eliasaph: eh-LYE-uh-saf

Eliashib: eh-LYE-uh-shib

Eliasib: eh-LYE-uh-sib

Eliasis: eh-LYE-uh-sis

Eliasub: eh-LYE-uh-suhb

Eliathah: eh-LYE-uh-thuh

Elica: eh-LYE-cuh

Elidad: eh-LYE-dad

Eliehoenai: eh-LYE-uh-hoh-**EE**-nye

Eliel: eh-LYE-ul

Eli Eli lama sabach-thani: EE-lye-EE-lye-LAH-muh-suh-**BAHK**-thuh-nee

Eli Eli lama sabachthani: EE-lye-EE-lye-LAH-muh-suh-**BAHK**-thuh-nee

Eli-Eli-lama-sabachthani: EE-lye-EE-lye-LAH-muh-suh-**BAHK**-thuh-nee

Elienai: EL-eh-**EE**-nye

Eliezar: EL-eh-**EE**-zuhr

Eliezer: EL-eh-**EE**-zuhr

Elihba: eh-LYE-uh-buh

Elihoenai: EL-eh-hoh-EE-nye

Elihoreph: el-eh-HOH-rif

Elihu: eh-LYE-hew

Elijah: eh-LYE-juh

Elika: eh-LYE-kuh

Elim: EE-lim

Elimelech: eh-LIM-uh-lek

Elimelek: eh-LIM-uh-lek

Elioda: el-EYE-uh-duh

Elioenai: EL-lee-oh-**EE**-nye

Elion: eh-LYE-uhn

Elionas: EL-ee-**OH**-nuhs

Eliphal: eh-LYE-fuhl

Eliphalat: eh-LIF-uh-lat

Eliphalet: eh-LIF-uh-let

Eliphaleth: el-LIFF-uh-leth

Eliphalu: eh-LIF-uh-luh

Eliphaz: EL-eh-faz

Elipheleh: eh-LIF-uh-luh

Eliphelehu: eh-LIF-uh-**LEE**-hew

Eliphelet: el-LIF-uh-let

Elipheleth: el-LIF-uh-leth

Elisa: eh-LYE-shuh

Elisabeth: eh-LIZ-uh-beth

Elisaeus: EL-uh-**SEE**-uhs or eh-LYE-see-uhs

Elisama: eh-LIS-eh-muh

Elisaphan: EL-uh-**ZAY**-fuhn

Eliseus: EL-uh-**SEE**-uhs or eh-LYE-see-uhs

Elisha: eh-LYE-shuh

Elishah: eh-LYE-shuh

Elishama: eh-LISH-uh-muh

Elishaphat: eh-LISH-uh-fat

Elisheba: eh-LISH-uh-buh

Elishua: EL-uh-**SHOO**-uh

Elisimus: eh-LIS-eh-muhs

Elisua: EL-uh-**SHOO**-uh

Elisur: eh-LYE-zuhr

Eliu: eh-LYE-yoo

Eliud: eh-LYE-uhd

Elizabeth: eh-LIZ-uh-beth

Elizaphan: EL-eh-**ZAY**-fan

Elizur: eh-LYE-zuhr

Eljehoenai: EL-juh-hoh-**EE**-nye

Elkanah: el-KAY-nuh

Elkesh: EL-kesh

Elkiah: el-KYE-uh

Elkohshite: EL-koh-shite

Elkosh: EL-kahsh

Elkoshite: EL-kahsh-ite

Ellasar: EL-uh-sahr

Elmadam: el-MAY-duhm

Elmelech. EL-muh-lek

Elmodad: el-MOH-dad

Elmodam: el-MOH-duhm

Elnaam: el-NAY-uhm

Elnaim: el-NAY-uhm

Elnathan: el-NAY-thuhn

Eloah: eh-LOH-uh

Elohe: el-OH-huh

Eloi: EE-loh-eye

Elon: EE-luhn

Elon Beth Hanan: EE-luhn-beth-**HAY**-nuhn

Elon Bethhanan: EE-luhn-beth-**HAY**-nuhn

Elon-beth-hanan: EE-luhn-beth-**HAY**-nuhn

Elon-bethhanan: EE-luhn-beth-**HAY**-nuhn

Elonbethhanan: EE-luhn-beth-**HAY**-nuhn

Elonite: EE-luh-nite

Elon-meonenim: EE-luhn-mee-**ON**-uh-nim

Eloth: EE-loth

Elpaal: el-PAY-uhl

Elpalet: el-PAY-lit

El Paran: el-PAY-ruhn

El-paran: el-PAY-ruhn

Elparan: el-PAY-ruhn

Elpelet: el-PEE-lit

Elphaal: el-PAY-ahl

Elteke: EL-tuh-kuh

Eltekeh: EL-tuh-kuh

Eltekoh: EL-tuh-koh

Eltekon: EL-tuh-kon

Eltheco: EL-tuh-koh

Eltecon: EL-tuh-kon

Elthece: EL-tuh-kuh

Eltholad: el-TOH-lad

Eltolad: el-TOH-lad

Elul: EE-luhl

Eluzai: el-YOO-zye

Elymaean: EL-uh-**MEE**-uhn

Elymais: EL-uh-**MAY**-uhs

Elymas: EL-uh-muhs

Elzabad: el-ZAY-bad

Elzaphan: el-ZAY-fan

Elzebad: el-ZAY-bad

Emadabun: eh-MAD-uh-buhn

Emalchuel: eh-MAL-kew-el

Eman: EE-muhn

Emath: EE-math

Emathis: EM-uh-thuhs

Emek: EE-mik

Emek Keziz: EE-mik-KEE-ziz

Emek-keziz: EE-mik-KEE-ziz

Emekkeziz: EE-mik-KEE-ziz

emerod: EM-uh-rod

Emim: EE-mim

Emite: EE-mite

Emmanuel: eh-MAN-yoo-el

Emmaus: eh-MAY-uhs

Emmer: EM-uhr

Emmor: EM-or

Emona: EM-oh-nuh

Emor: EM-or

En: en

Enac: EE-nak

Enacim: AN-uh-kuhm

Enaim: eh-NAY-im

Enam: EE-nuhm

Enan: EE-nuhn

Enasibus: eh-NAS-uh-buhs

En Dor: EN-dor

En-dor: EN-dor

Endor: EN-dor

Eneas: eh-NEE-uhs

En Eglaim: en-EG-lay-im

En-eglaim: en-EG-lay-im

Eneglaim: en-EG-lay-im

Enemessar: EN-uh-**MES**-uhr

Enenius: eh-NEN-ee-uhs

Engaddi: en-GAD-eye

Engallim: en-EG-lay-im

En Gannim: en-GAN-im

En-gannim: en-GAN-im

Engannim: en-GAN-im

En Gedi: en-GED-eye

En-gedi: en-GED-eye

Engedi: en-GED-eye

En Hadda: en-HAD-uh

En-hadda: en-HAD-uh

En-haddah: en-HAD-uh

Enhadda: en-HAD-uh

En Hakkore: en-HAK-uh-ree

En-hakkore: en-HAK-uh-ree

Enhakkore: en-HAK-uh-ree

En-harod: en-HAIR-ahd

Enhasor: en-HAY-zahr

En Hazor: en-HAY-zahr

En-hazor: en-HAY-zahr

Enhazor: en-HAY-zahr

En Mishpat: en-MISH-pat

En-mishpat: en-MISH-pat

Enmishpat: en-MISH-pat

Ennom: EN-uhm

Enoch: EE-nuhk

Enon: EE-nuhn

Enos: EE-nuhs

Enosh: EE-nahsh

En Rimmon: en-RIM-uhn

En-rimmon: en-RIM-uhn

Enrimmon: en-RIM-uhn

En Rogel: en-ROH-guhl

En-rogel: en-ROH-guhl

Enrogel: en-ROH-guhl

Ensemes: en-SEM-is

En Shemesh: en-SHEM-ish

En-shemesh: en-SHEM-ish

Enshemesh: en-SHEM-ish

En Tappuah: en-TAP-yoo-uh

En-tappuah: en-TAP-yoo-uh

Entappuah: en-TAP-yoo-uh

Epaenetus: eh-PEE-nuh-tuhs

Epaphras: EP-uh-fras

Epaphroditus: eh-PAF-ruh-**DYE**-tuhs

Epeiph: EE-fyef

Epenetus: eh-PEE-nuh-tuhs

Epha: EE-fuh

Ephah: EE-fuh

ephah: EE-fuh

Ephai: EE-fye

Epher: EE-fuhr

Ephes Dammim: EE-fiz-**DAM**-im

Ephes-dammim: EE-fiz-**DAM**-im

Ephesdammim: EE-fiz-**DAM**-im

Ephes Dammin: EE-fiz-**DAM**-in

Ephesian: eh-FEE-zhuhn

Ephesus: EF-uh-suhs

ephi: EE-fye

Ephlal: EF-lal

Ephod: EE-fahd

ephod: EE-fahd

ephphatha: EF-uh-thuh

Ephra: EF-ruh

Ephraim: EE-frah-im

Ephraimite: EE-fray-uh-mite

Ephrain: EE-fray-in

Ephrata: EF-ruh-tuh

Ephratah: EF-ruh-tuh

Ephrath: EF-rath

Ephratha: EF-ruh-thuh

Ephrathah: EF-ruh-thuh

Ephrathite: EF-ruh-thite

Ephron: EE-frahn

Epicurean: EP-eh-kew-**REE**-uhn

Epiphanes: eh-PIF-uh-neez

Epiphi: EP-eh-fye

Epistle: eh-PIS-uhl

Er: uhr

Eran: EER-an

Eranite: EER-uh-nite

Erastus: eh-RAS-tuhs

Erech: EE-rek

Eri: EE-rye

ericius: eh-RIS-ee-uhs

Erite: EE-rite

Esaan: ES-ee-uhn

Esaias: eh-ZAY-uhs

Esar-haddon: EE-sahr-**HAD**-uhn

Esarhaddon: EE-sahr-**HAD**-uhn

Esau: EE-saw

Esbaal: es-BAY-uhl

Esbon: EZ-bahn

Escol: ES-kahl

Esdraelon: EZ-druh-**EE**-luhn

Esdras: EZ-druhs

Esdrias: EZ-drye-uhs

Esdrin: EZ-drin

Esdris: EZ-dris

Eseban: ES-eh-bahn

Esebon: ES-eh-bahn

Esebrias: ES-eh-**BRYE**-uhs

Esec: EE-sehk

Esek: EE-sehk

Esem: EE-zem

Eser: EE-zuhr

Eshan: EE-shuhn

Esh-baal: esh-BAY-uhl

Eshbaal: esh-BAY-uhl

Esh-ban: ESH-ban

Eshban: ESH-ban

Eshcol: ESH-kahl

Eshean: ESH-ee-uhn

Eshek: EE-shek

Eshkalonite: ESH-kuh-luh-nite

Eshtaol: ESH-tay-uhl

Eshtaolite: ESH-tay-uh-lite

Eshtarah: ESH-tuh-ruh

Eshtaulite: ESH-tuh-**YOO**-lite

Eshtemoa: ESH-tuh-**MOH**-uh

Eshtemoh: ESH-tuh-moh

Eshton: ESH-tahn

Esli: ES-lye

Esna: ES-nuh

Esora: eh-SOR-uh

Esra: EZ-ruh

Esriel: EZ-ree-el

Esril: ES-ril

Esrom: ES-rahm

Esron: ES-rahn

Estaol: ES-tay-uhl

Estemo: ES-tuh-moh

Ester: ES-tuhr

Esthamo: ES-thuh-moh

Esthamoa: ES-thuh-**MOH**-uh

Esthaol: ES-thay-al

Esthaolite: ES-thah-**OH**-lite

Esthemo: ES-thuh-moh

Esther: ES-tuhr

Esthon: ES-thahn

Etam: EE-tum

Ethai: eh-THAY-eye

Etham: EE-thuhm

Ethan: EE-thuhn

Ethanim: ETH-uh-nim

Ethanus: eh-THAY-nuhs

Ethbaal: eth-BAY-uhl

Ethei: ETH-eye

Ether: EE-thuhr

Ethi: ETH-eye

Ethiopia: EE-thee-**OH**-pee-uh

Ethiopian: EE-thee-**OH**-pee-uhn

Eth Kazin: eth-KAY-zin

Eth-kazin: eth-KAY-zin

Ethkazin: eth-KAY-zin

Ethma: ETH-muh

Ethnan: ETH-nuhn

Ethnarch: ETH-nahrk

Ethni: ETH-nye

Etroth: ET-rahth

Eubulus: yoo-BEW-luhs

Euergetes: yoo-UHR-juh-teez

Eumenes: YOO-muh-neez

Eunatan: yoo-NAY-tuhn

Eunice: YOO-nis

eunuch: YOO-nuhk

Euodia: yoo-OH-dee-uh

Euodias: yoo-OH-dee-uhs

Eupator: yoo-PAY-tor

Euphrates: yoo-FRAY-teez

Eupolemus: yoo-POL-uh-muhs

Eurakylon: yoo-RAHK-eh-lahn

Euraquila: yoo-RAHK-wi-luh

Euraquilo: yoo-RAWK-wi-loh

Euroclydon: yoo-RAHK-li-don

Eutychus: YOO-tuh-kuhs

Evangelist: eh-VAN-juh-list

Eve: eev

Evi: EE-vye

Evil-merodach: EE-vuhl-**MAIR**-uh-dak

Evilmerodach: EE-vuhl-**MAIR**-uh-dak

Evodia: eh-VOH-dee-uh

Exodus: EK-suh-duhs

Ezar: EE-zuhr

Ezbai: EZ-bye

Ezbon: EZ-bahn

Ezechias: EZ-uh-**KYE**-uhs

Ezechiel: eh-ZEE-kee-uhl

Ezecias: EZ-uh-**KYE**-uhs

Ezekias: EZ-uh-**KYE**-uhs

Ezekiel: eh-ZEE-kee-uhl

Ezel: EE-zuhl

Ezem: EE-zuhm

Ezer: EE-zuhr

Ezerias: EZ-uh-**RYE**-uhs

Ezias: eh-ZYE-uhs

Ezion-gaber: EE-zee-uhn-**GAY**-buhr

Ezion Geber: EE-zee-uhn-**GEE**-buhr

Ezion-geber: EE-zee-uhn-**GEE**-buhr

Eziongeber: EE-zee-uhn-**GEE**-buhr

Eznite: EZ-nite

Ezora: eh-ZOR-uh

Ezra: EZ-ruh

Ezrah: EZ-ruh

Ezrahite: EZ-ruh-hite

Ezra-Nehemyah: EZ-ruh-neh-**HEM**-yuh

Ezri: EZ-rye

Ezricam: EZ-ruh-kam

Ezriel: EZ-ree-el

Ezrite: EZ-rite

F

Fair Havens: fair-HAY-vins

fauchion: FAW-chuhn

Felix: FEE-liks

felloe: FEL-oh

Festus: FES-tuhs

firkin: FUHR-kin

Fortunatus: FOR-chuh-**NAY**-tuhs

frumenty: FROO-muhn-tee

G

Gaal: GAY-uhl

Gaas: GAY-as

Gaash: GAY-ash

Gaba: GAY-buh

Gabaa: GAB-ay-uh

Gabaath: GAB-ay-uhth

Gabae: GAB-ay-uh

Gabael: GAB-ay-uhl

Gabam: GAY-buhm

Gabaon: GAB-ay-uhn

Gabatha: GAB-uh-thuh

Gabathon: GAB-uh-thuhn

Gabbai: GAB-eye

Gabbatha: GAB-uh-thuh

Gabdes: GAB-deez

Gabee: GAB-ee-uh

Gaber: GAY-ber

Gabim: GAY-bim

Gaboes: GAY-bohz

Gabrias: GAY-bree-uhs

Gabriel: GAY-bree-uhl

Gad: gad

Gadara: GAD-uh-ruh

Gadarene: GAD-uh-reen

Gaddah: GAD-uh

Gaddi: GAD-eye

Gaddiel: GAD-ee-uhl

Gaddis: GAD-is

Gader: GAY-duhr

Gaderoth: guh-DEER-ahth

Gadgad: GAD-gad

Gadi: GAY-dye

Gadite: GAD-ite

Gador: GAY-dor

Gaham: GAY-ham

Gahar: GAY-hahr

Gaher: GAY-huhr

Gai: gye

Gaius: GAY-uhs

Galaad: GAL-ay-uhd

Galal: GAY-lal

Galatia: guh-LAY-shuh

Galatian: guh-LAY-shuhn

galbanum: GAL-buh-nuhm

Galeed: GAL-ee-ed

Galgal: GAL-gal

Galgala: GAL-guh-luh

Galilaean: GAL-uh-**LEE**-uhn

Galilean: GAL-uh-**LEE**-uhn

Galilee: GAL-uh-lee

Gallim: GAL-im

Gallio: GAL-ee-oh

Gallium: GAL-ee-uhm

Gamad: GAY-mad

Gamadite: GAY-muh-dite

Gamael: GAM-ay-uhl

Gamaliel: guh-MAY-lee-uhl

Gammad: GAM-uhd

Gammadim: GAM-uh-dim

Gamul: GAY-muhl

Gannim: GAN-im

Gar: gahr

Garazim: GAIR-uh-zim

Gareb: GAIR-ib

Garizim: GAIR-uh-zim

Garmi: GAR-mye

Garmite: GAHR-mite

Gas: gas

Gashmu: GASH-mew

Gatam: GAY-tuhm

Gath: gath

Gathan: GAY-thuhn

Gath Hepher: gath-HEE-fuhr

Gath-hepher: gath-HEE-fuhr

Gathhepher: gath-HEE-fuhr

Gather: GATH-uhr

Gathite: GATH-ite

Gath Rimmon: gath-RIM-uhn

Gath-rimmon: gath-RIM-uhn

Gathrimmon: gath-RIM-uhn

Gaul: gawl

Gaulanitis: GAWL-uh-**NYE**-tis

Gaulon: GAWL-uhn

Gaver: GAV-uhr

Gaza: GAH-zuh or GAY-zuh

Gazan: GAH-zuhn or GAY-zuhn

Gazara: guh-ZAY-ruh

Gazathite: GAY-zuh-thite

Gazer: GAY-zer

Gazera: guh-ZEE-ruh

Gazez: GAY-ziz

Gazite: GAY-zite

Gazzam: GAZ-uhm

Gazzan: GAZ-uhn

Geba: GEE-buh

Gebal: GEE-bul

Gebalite: GEE-buh-lite

Gebbethon: GIB-uh-thuhn

Geber: GEE-buhr

Gebim: GEE-bim

gecko: GEK-oh

Gedaliah: GED-uh-**LYE**-uh

Geddiel: GED-ee-uhl

Geddur: GED-uhr

Gedelias: GED-uh-**LYE**-uhs

Gedeon: GED-ee-uhn

Geder: GEE-duhr

Gedera: geh-DEE-ruh

Gederah: geh-DEE-ruh

Gederathite: guh-DEE-ruh-thite

Gederite: geh-DEE-rite

Gederoth: geh-DEE-rahth

Gederothaim: guh-DEE-ruh-**THAY**-im

Gedi: GED-eye

Gedor: GEE-dohr

Geennom: geh-EN-uhm

Ge Harashim: geh-HAIR-uh-shim

Ge-harashim: geh-HAIR-uh-shim

Geharashim: geh-HAIR-uh-shim

Gehazi: geh-HAY-zye

Gehenna: geh-HEN-uh

Ge-hinnom: geh-HIN-uhm

Gehon: GEE-hohn

Gelboe: gel-BOH-uh

Geliloth: geh-LYE-lahth

Gelonite: GEL-uh-nite

Gemalli: geh-MAL-eye

Gemariah: GEM-uh-**RYE**-uh

Gamarias: GEM-uh-**RYE**-uh

Genesar: geh-NEE-sahr

Genesis: JEN-uh-sis

Gennaeus: geh-NEE-uhs

Gennesar: geh-NEE-sahr

Gennesaret: geh-NES-uh-ret

Genessareth: geh-NES-uh-reth

Genneus: geh-NEE-uhs

Gentile: JEN-tile

Genubath: geh-NEW-bath

Geon: GEE-on

Gera: GEE-ruh

Gerah: GEE-ruh

gerah: GEE-ruh

Gerar: GEE-rahr

Gerara: gee-RAHR-uh

Gerasa: GER-uh-suh

Gerasene: GER-uh-seen

Gergesene: GER-guh-seen

Gergesite: GER-guh-site

Gergezite: GER-guh-zite

Gerizim: GER-uh-zim

Geron: GEER-on

Gerrene: guh-REE-nee

Gerrenian: guh-REE-nee-uhn

Gerrhenian: guh-REE-nee-uhn

Gersam: GER-suhm

Gershom: GER-shuhm

Gershomite: GER-shuh-mite

Gershon: GER-shuhn

Gershonite: GER-shuh-nite

Gersom: GER-suhm

Gerson: GER-suhn

Geruth Chimham: GEER-ooth-**KIM**-ham

Geruth Kimham: GEER-ooth-**KIM**-ham

Gerzi: GER-zye

Gerzite: GER-zite

Gesan: GEE-suhn

Gesem: GEE-suhm

Gesham: GEE-shuhm

Geshan: GESH-uhn

Geshem: GESH-uhm

Geshur: GESH-uhr

Geshuri: geh-SHOOR-eye

Geshurite: GESH-uh-rite

Gessen: GES-uhn

Gessur: GES-uhr

Gessuri: geh-SOOR-eye

Geth: geth

Gethaim: geh-THAY-im

Gether: GEE-thuhr

Gethhepher: gath-HEE-fuhr

Gethite: GETH-ite

Gethrite: GETH-rite

Gethremmon: geth-REM-muhn

Gethsemane: geth-SEM-uh-nee

Geuel: GEW-uhl

Gezer: GEE-zuhr

Gezeron: GEE-zuhr-on

Gezez: GEE-zez

Gezonite: GEZ-uhn-ite

Gezrite: GEZ-rite

ghimel: GIM-uhl

Giah: GYE-uh

Gibbar: GIB-ahr

Gibbeah: GIB-ee-uh

Gibbeath: GIB-ee-uhth

Gibbethon: GIB-uh-thon

Gibea: GIB-ee-uh

Gibeah: GIB-ee-uh

Gibeath: GEB-ee-uhth

Gibeath-elohim: GIB-ee-uhth-**EL**-oh-him

Gibeathelohim: GIB-ee-uhth-**EL**-oh-him

Gibeath Haaraloth: GIB-ee-uhth-hay-**AIR**-uh-loth

Gibeath-haaraloth: GIB-ee-uhth-hay-**AIR**-uh-loth

Gibeath-ha-araloth: GIB-ee-uhth-hay-**AIR**-uh-loth

Gibeath-hammoreh: GIB-ee-uhth-hah-**MOR**-uh

Gibeathite: GIB-ee-uh-thite

Gibeon: GIB-ee-uhn

Gibeonite: GIB-ee-uh-nite

Giblite: GIB-lite

Giddalti: geh-DAL-tye

Giddel: GID-uhl

Gideon: GID-ee-uhn

Gideoni: GID-ee-**OH**-nye

Gideroth: gid-EE-ruhth

Gidgad: GID-gad

Gidom: GI-duhm

gier: jeer

Giezi: geh-EE-zye

Gihon: GYE-hahn

Gilalai: GIL-uh-lye

Gilboa: gil-BOH-uh

Gilead: GIL-ee-uhd

Gileadite: GIL-ee-uh-dite

Gilgal: GIL-gal

Gilo: GYE-loh

Giloh: GYE-loh

Gilonite: GYE-luh-nite

gimel: GIM-uhl

Gimzo: GIM-zoh

Ginath: GYE-nath

Gineth: GYE-neth

Ginnetho: GIN-uh-thoh

Ginnethoi: GIN-uh-thoi

Ginnethon: GIN-uh-thon

Girgashite: GER-guh-shite

Girgasite: GER-guh-site

Girgesite: GER-guh-site

Girzite: GER-zyte

Gishpa: GISH-puh

Gispa: GIS-puh

Gittah-hepher: GIT-uh-**HEE**-fuhr

Gittaim: GIT-ay-im

Gittite: GIT-tite

Gittith: GIT-ith

Gizonite: GEH-zoh-nite

Gizrite: GIZ-rite

glede: gleed

Gnidus: NYE-duhs

Goah: GOH-uh

Goath: GOH-ath

Goatha: GOH-ath-uh

Gob: gahb

God: gahd

Godhead: GAHD-hed

Godolias: GAHD-uh-**LYE**-uhs

Gog: gahg

Goiim: GOI-im

Golan: GOH-luhn

Golgotha: GAHL-guh-thuh or gahl-GAH-thuh

Goliath: guh-LYE-uhth

Gomer: GOH-muhr

Gomorrah: guh-MOHR-uh

Gomorrha: guh-MOHR-uh

Goren-ha-atad: GOR-in-hah-AY-tad

Gorgias: GOR-juhs

Gortyn: GOR-tin

Gortyna: gor-TYE-nuh

Gosen: GOH-sen

Goshen: GOH-shuhn

Gospel: GOS-puhl

Gotholiah: GOTH-uh-LYE-uh

Gotholias: GOTH-uh-LYE-uhs

Gothoniel: goh-THAHN-ee-uhl

Goyim: GOI-im

Gozan: GOH-zan

Gozen: GOH-zuhn

Graba: GRAH-buh

Grecia: GREE-shuh

Grecian: GREE-shuhn

Greece: grees

Greek: greek

grype: gripe

Gudgodah: gud-GOH-duh

Guel: GEW-uhl

Guni: GEW-nye

Gunite: GEW-nite

Gur: guhr

Gur Baal: guhr-BAY-uhl

Gur-baal: guhr-BAY-uhl

Gurbaal: guhr-BAY-uhl

H

Haahashtari: HAY-uh-**HASH**-tuh-rye

Haammonai: hay-AM-uh-nye

Haba: HAHB-uh

Habacuc: HAB-uh-kuhk

habaiah: huh-BAY-uh

Habakkuk: huh-BAK-uhk

Habaziniah: HAB-uh-zuh-**NYE**-uh

Habazziniah: HAB-uh-zuh-**NYE**-uh

Habbacuc: huh-BAK-uhk

Haber: HAY-buhr

habergeon: HAB-uhr-juhn

Habor: HAY-bor

Habucuc: HAB-uh-kuhk

Habsanias: HAB-zuh-**NYE**-uhs

Hacaliah: HAK-uh-**LYE**-uh

Haccerem: HAK-uh-rem

Hachaliah: HAK-uh-**LYE**-uh

Hachamoni: HAK-uh-**MOH**-nye

Hachila: huh-KYE-luh

Hachilah: huh-KYE-luh

Hachmon: HAK-muhn

Hachmoni: HAK-moh-nye

Hachmonite: HAK-moh-nite

Hacmoni: HAK-moh-nye

Hacmonite: HAK-moh-nite

Hadad: HAY-dad

Hadadezer: HAY-dad-**EE**-zuhr

Hadarezer: HAD-uhr-**EE**-zuhr

Hadad Rimmon: HAY-dad-**RIM**-uhn

Hadadrimmon: HAY-dad-**RIM**-uhn

Hadaia: huh-DYE-uh

Hadar: HAY-dahr

Hadarezer: HAY-duhr-**EE**-zuhr

Hadashah: huh-DASH-uh

Hadassa: huh-DAS-uh

Hadassah: huh-DAS-uh

Hadatta: huh-DAT-uh

Haddah: HAD-uh

Haddon: HAD-uhn

Hades: HAY-deez

Hadid: HAY-did

Hadlai: HAD-lye

Hadoram: huh-DOR-uhm

Hadrach: HAD-rak

Hadrak: HAD-rak

Hadriel: HAY-dree-uhl

Haeleph: hay-EE-lehf

Hagab: HAY-gab

Hagaba: HAG-uh-buh

Hagabah: HAG-uh-buh

Hagar: HAY-gahr

Hagarene: HAG-uh-reen

Hagarite: HAG-uh-rite

Hagerite: HAG-uh-rite

Haggadol: HAG-uh-dahl

Haggai: HAG-eye

Haggedolim: HAG-uh-**DOH**-lim

Haggeri: HAG-uh-rye

Haggi: HAG-ee

Haggia: hag-EYE-uh

Haggiah: hag-EYE-uh

Haggite: HAG-ite

Haggith: HAG-ith

Hagia: HAY-gee-uh

Hagri: HAG-rye

Hagrite: HAG-rite

Hahiroth: huh-HYE-rahth

Hai: hye

Hakeldama: huh-KEL-duh-muh

Hakilah: huh-KYE-luh

Hakkatan: HAK-uh-tan

Hakkore: HAK-uh-ree

Hakkoz: HAK-ahz

Hakupha: huh-KEW-fuh

Hala: HAY-luh

Halaa: huh-LAY-uh

Halah: HAY-luh

Halak: HAY-lak

Halcath: HAL-kath

Halhul: HAL-huhl

Hali: HAY-lye

Halicarnassus: HAL-uh-kahr-**NAS**-uhs

hallel: HAL-el

halleluhah: HAL-uh-**LOO**-yuh

Hallohesh: huh-LOH-hesh

Halohesh: huh-LOH-hesh

Ham: ham

Haman: HAY-muhn

Hamath: HAY-muth

Hamathite: HAY-muh-thite

Hamath Zobah: HAY-math-**ZOH**-buh

Hamath-zobah: HAY-math-**ZOH**-buh

Hamathzobah: HAY-math-**ZOH**-buh

Hamite: HAM-ite

Hammahlekoth: huh-MAH-li-kahth

Hammath: HAM-ath

Hammedatha: HAM-uh-**DAY**-thuh

Hammelech: HAM-uh-lek

Hammolecheth: ha-MAHL-uh-keth

Hammoleketh: ha-MAHL-uh-keth
Hammon: HAM-uhn
Hammoth Dor: HAM-muhth-dor
Hammoth-dor: HAM-muhth-dor
Hammothdor: HAM-muhth-dor
Hammuel: HAM-yoo-uhl
Hamon: HAY-muhn
Hamonah: huh-MOH-nuh
Hamon Gog: HAY-muhn-**GOG**
Hamon-gog: HAY-muhn-**GOG**
Hamongog: HAY-muhn-**GOG**
Hamor: HAY-mor
Hamram: HAM-ram
Hamran: HAM-ran
Hamuel: HAM-you-uhl
Hamul: HAY-muhl
Hamulite: HAY-muh-lite
Hamutal: huh-MEW-tuhl
Hana: HAY-nuh
Hanameel: huh-NAM-ee-uhl
Hanamel: HAN-uh-mel
Hanan: HAY-nuhn
Hananeal: huh-NAN-ee-uhl
Hananeel: HAN-uh-neel
Hananel: HAN-uh-nel
Hanani: huh-NAY-nye
Hanania: HAN-uh-**NYE**-uh
Hananiah: HAN-uh-**NYE**-uh
Hananias: HAN-uh-**NYE**-uhs
Hananiel: huh-NAN-ee-uhl
Hanathon: HAN-uh-thahn
Hanes: HAY-neez
Haniel: HAN-ee-uhl
Hannah: HAN-uh
Hannathon: HAN-uh-thahn

Hanniel: HAN-ee-uhl

Hanoch: HAY-nahk

Hanochite: HAY-nuh-kite

Hanok: HAY-nahk

Hanon: HAY-nuhn

Hanun: HAY-nuhn

Hapham: HAHP-him

Hapharaim: haf-uh-RAY-im

Haphraim: haf-RAY-im

Haphsiba: HAF-zib-uh

Happhim: HAP-him

Happizzez: HAP-uh-zez

Happuch: HAP-uhk

Hara: HAIR-uh

Harad: HAY-red

Haradah: huh-RAY-duh

Haran: HAIR-uhn

Harar: HAIR-uhr

Hararite: HAIR-uh-rite

Harbel: HAHR-bel

Harbona: hahr-BOH-nuh

Harbonah: hahr-BOH-nuh

Harel: HAIR-uhl

Hareph: HAIR-if

Hares: HAIR-ez

Haresha: huh-REE-shuh

Haret: HAIR-et

Hareth: HAIR-eth

Harhaiah: hahr-HAY-uh

Harhas: HAHR-has

Har-heres: hahr-HEER-ez

Harheres: hahr-HEER-ez

Harhur: HAHR-huhr

Harim: HAIR-im

Hariph: HAIR-if

Har-magedon: HAHR-muh-**GED**-uhn

Harma: HAHR-muh

Harmon: HAHR-muhn

Harnepher: HAHR-nuh-fer

Harod: HAIR-uhd

Harodi: huh-ROH-dye

Harodite: HAIR-uh-dite

Haroeh: huh-ROH-uh

Harorite: HAY-roh-rite

Haroseth: huh-ROH-sheth

Harosheth: huh-ROH-sheth

Harosheth Haggoyim: huh-ROH-sheth-huh-**GOI**-im

Harosheth-ha-goiim: huh-ROH-sheth-huh-**GOI**-im

Harosheth-hagoiim: huh-ROH-sheth-huh-**GOI**-im

Haroshethhagoiim: huh-ROH-sheth-huh-**GOI**-im

Harosheth Hagoyim: huh-ROH-sheth-huh-**GOI**-im

Harosheth-hagoyim: huh-ROH-sheth-huh-**GOI**-im

Harsa: HAHR-suh

Harsha: HAHR-shuh

Harsith: HAHR-sith

Harum: HAIR-uhm

Harumaph: huh-ROO-maf

Haruphite: huh-ROO-fite

Harus: HAIR-uhz

Haruz: HAIR-uhz

Hasaba: huh-SAY-buh

Hasabia: HAS-uh-**BYE**-uh

Hasadiah: HAS-uh-**DYE**-uh

Hasadias: HAS-uh-**DYE**-uhs

Hasarsuhal: HAY-sahr-**SOO**-huhl

Hasarsusim: HAY-sahr-**SOO**-sim

Hasebia: HAS-uh-**BYE**-uh

Hasenuah: HAS-uh-**NOO**-uh

Haserim: HAY-zuhr-im

Haseroth: ha-ZEE-rahth

Hasersual: HAY-zuhr-**SOO**-uhl

Hasersusa: HAY-zuhr-**SOO**-suh

Hash: hash

Hashabiah: HASH-uh-**BYE**-uh

Hashabnah: huh-SHAB-nuh

Hashabneah: HASH-uhb-**NEE**-uh

Hashabneiah: HASH-uhb-**NEE**-uh

Hashabniah: HASH-uhb-**NYE**-uh

Hashbadana: hash-BAD-uh-nuh

Hashbaddanah: hash-BAD-uh-nuh

Hashem: HAY-shem

Hashmonah: hash-MOH-nuh

Hashub: HAY-shuhb

Hashubah: huh-SHOO-buh

Hashum: HAY-shuhm

Hashupha: huh-SHOO-fuh

Hasidaean: HAS-uh-**DEE**-uhn

Hasidean: HAS-uh-**DEE**-uhn

Hasim: HAY-sim

Hasor: HAY-zor

Hasrah: HAZ-ruh

Hassemon: HAS-uh-mahn

Hassenaah: HAS-uh-**NAY**-uh

Hassenuah: HAS-uh-**NOO**-uh

Hasshub: HASH-uhb

Hassophereth: ha-SOF-uh-reth

Hassub: HAS-oob

Hasupha: huh-SOO-fuh

Hatach: HAY-tak

Hathath: HAY-thath

Hatita: huh-TYE-tuh

Hattaavah: huh-TAY-uh-vah

Hatticon: HAT-uh-kon

Hattil: HAT-uhl

Hattus: HAT-uhs

Hattush: HAT-uhsh

Hauran: HAW-ruhn

Havilah: HAV-uh-luh

Havilah-by-shur: HAV-uh-luh-bye-**SHUHR**

Havoth: HAY-vahth

Havoth-Jair: HAY-vahth-**JAY**-uhr

Havvoth Jair: HAV-ahth-**JAY**-uhr

Havvoth-jair: HAV-ahth-**JAY**-uhr

Havvothjair: HAV-ahth-**JAY**-uhr

Hayamim: hay-YAH-mim

Hazael: HAY-zay-uhl

Hazaiah: huh-ZAY-uh

Hazar: HAY-zuhr

Hazar Addar: HAY-zuhr-**AD**-uhr

Hazar-addar: HAY-zuhr-**AD**-uhr

Hazaraddar: HAY-zuhr-**AD**-uhr

Hazar Enan: HAY-zuhr-**EE**-nuhn

Hazar-enan: HAY-zuhr-**EE**-nuhn

Hazarenan: HAY-zuhr-**EE**-nuhn

Hazar-enon: HAY-zuhr-**EE**-nuhn

Hazarenon: HAY-zuhr-**EE**-nuhn

Hazar Gaddah: HAY-zuhr-**GAD**-uh

Hazar-gaddah: HAY-zuhr-**GAD**-uh

Hazargaddah: HAY-zuhr-**GAD**-uh

Hazar Hatticon: HAY-zuhr-**HAT**-uh-kahn

Hazar-hatticon: HAY-zuhr-**HAT**-uh-kahn

Hazar-maveth: HAY-zuhr-**MAY**-veth

Hazarmaveth: HAY-zuhr-**MAY**-veth

Hazar Shual: HAY-zuhr-**SHOO**-uhl

Hazar-shual: HAY-zuhr-**SHOO**-uhl

Hazarshual: HAY-zuhr-**SHOO**-uhl

Hazar Susah: HAY-zuhr-**SOO**-suh

Hazar-susah: HAY-zuhr-**SOO**-suh

Hazarsusah: HAY-zuhr-**SOO**-suh

Hazar Susim: HAY-zuhr-**SOO**-sim

Hazar-susim: HAY-zuhr-**SOO**-sim

Hazarsusim: HAY-zuhr-**SOO**-sim

Hazazon: HAZ-uh-zahn

Hazazon Tamar: HAZ-uh-zahn-**TAY**-muhr

Hazazon-tamar: HAZ-uh-zahn-**TAY**-muhr

Hazazontamar: HAZ-uh-zahn-**TAY**-muhr

Hazelelponi: HAZ-uh-lel-**POH**-nye

Hazer Hatticon: HAY-zuhr-**HAT**-uh-kahn

Hazer-hatticon: HAY-zuhr-**HAT**-uh-kahn

Hazerhatticon: HAY-zuhr-**HAT**-uh-kahn

Hazerim: huh-ZEER-im

Hazeroth: huh-ZEER-ahth

Hazezon Tamar: HAZ-uh-zahn-**TAY**-muhr

Hazezon-tamar: HAZ-uh-zahn-**TAY**-muhr

Haziel: HAY-zee-uhl

Hazo: HAY-zoh

Hazor: HAY-zor

Hazor Hadattah: HAY-zor-huh-**DAT**-uh

Hazor-hadattah: HAY-zor-huh-**DAT**-uh

Hazorhadattah: HAY-zor-huh-**DAT**-uh

Hazzebaim: HAZ-uh-**BAY**-im

Hazzelelponi: HAZ-uh-lel-**POH**-nye

Hazzobebah: HAZ-oh-**BEE**-buh

Hazzurim: HAZ-uh-rim

he: hay

Hebal: HEE-buhl

Heber: HEE-buhr

Heberite: HEE-buh-rite

Hebrew: HEE-broo

Hebrewess: HEE-broo-es

Hebron: HEE-bruhn

Hebrona: huh-BRO-nuh

Hebroni: HEE-bruhn-eye

Hebronite: HEE-bruh-nite

Heddai: HID-ay-eye

Heder: HEE-duhr

Hegai: HEG-eye

Hege: HEE-gee

Hegemonides: HEJ-uh-**MOH**-nuh-deez

Hegla: HEG-luh

Heglam: HEG-luhm

Helah: HEE-luh

Helam: HEE-luhm

Helba: HEL-buh

Helbah: HEL-buh

Helbon: HEL-bon

Helcath: HEL-kath

Helchiah: hel-KYE-uh

Helcias: hel-KYE-uhs

Heldai: HEL-dye

Heleb: HEE-leb

Helec: HEE-lek

Helech: HEE-lek

Heled: HEE-led

Helek: HEE-lek

Helekite: HEE-luh-kite

Helem: HEE-lem

Heleph: HEE-lef

Heler: HEE-luhr

Heles: HEE-lez

Helez: HEE-lez

Heli: HEE-lye

Helias: HEE-lee-uhs

Heliodorus: HEE-lee-uh-**DOR**-uhs

Heliopolis: HEE-lee-**AHP**-uh-lis

Helisur: he-LYE-zuhr

Helkai: HEL-kye

Helkath: HEL-kath

Helkath Hazzurim: HEL-kath-**HAZ**-yoo-rim

Helkath-hazzurim: HEL-kath-**HAZ**-yoo-rim

Helkathhazzurim: HEL-kath-**HAZ**-yoo-rim

Helkias: hel-KYE-uhs

Hellenism: **HEL**-uh-NIZ-uhm

Hellenist: HEL-uh-nist

Hellenistic: HEL-uh-**NIS**-tik

Hellenization: HEL-uh-nye-**ZAY**-shuhn

Helles: HEE-lez

Hellez: HEL-iz

Helmondeblathaim: HEL-muhn-DIB-luh-**THAY**-im

Helon: HEE-lahn

Helper: HELP-uhr

Hem: hehm

Hemam: HEE-mam

Heman: HEE-muhn

Hemath: HEE-math

Hemdan: HEM-dan

Hemor: HEE-mahr

Hen: hen

Hena: HEN-uh

Henadad: HEN-uh-dad

Henoc: HEE-nuhk

Henoch: HEE-nuhk

Henochite: HEE-nuhk-ite

Hepher: HEE-fuhr

Hepherite: HEE-fuh-rite

Hephzi-bah: HEF-zi-buh

Hephzibah: HEF-zi-buh

Heradonijah: huhr-AD-uh-**NYE**-juh

Her: huhr

Heran: HEE-ran

Hercules: HUHR-kew-leez

Hered: HAHR-uhd

Heredite: HAHR-uh-dite

Herem: HAHR-uhm

Heres: HEER-ez

Heresh: HEER-esh

Hereth: HEER-eth

Hermas: HUHR-muhs

Hermes: HUHR-meez

Hermogenes: huhr-MAHJ-uh-neez

Hermon: HUHR-muhn

Hermonite: HUHR-muh-nite

Hernapher: HUHR-nuh-fuhr

Herod: HAIR-uhd

Herodian: heh-ROH-dee-uhn

Herodias: heh-ROH-dee-uhs

Herodion: heh-ROH-dee-uhn

Hesebon: HES-uh-bahn

Hesed: HEE-sed

Heser: HEE-zuhr

Heshbon: HESH-bahn

Heshbonite: HESH-buh-nite

Heshmon: HESH-mahn

Hesli: HES-lye

Hesmona: hes-MOH-nuh

Hesrai: HEZ-rye

Hesro: HEZ-roh

Hesron: HEZ-ruhn

Heth: Heth

heth: hayth

Hethite: HIT-ite

Hethalon: HETH-uh-lon

Hethlon: HETH-lon

Hevi: HEE-vye

Hevila: HAV-uh-luh

Hevite: HEE-vite

Hezeci: HEZ-uh-kye

Hezeki: HEZ-uh-kye

Hezekiah: HEZ-uh-KYE-uh

Hezion: HEE-zee-uhn

Hezir: HEE-zuhr

Hezrai: HEZ-rye

Hezro: HEZ-roh

Hezron: HEZ-ron

Hezronite: HEZ-ruh-nite

Hiddai: HID-eye

Hiddekel: HID-uh-kel

Hiel: HYE-uhl

Hierapolis: HYE-uh-**RAP**-uh-lis

Hiereel: hye-EER-ee-uhl

Hieremoth: hye-EER-uh-moth

Hierielus: hi-EER-eh-**EE**-luhs

Hiermas: hye-UHR-muhs

Hieronymus: hye-uh-RON-uh-muhs

Higgaion: hye-GAY-uhn

Higgayon: hye-GAY-uhn

Hilen: HYE-luhn

Hilkath: HIL-kath

Hilkiah: HEL-kye-uh

Hillel: HIL-uhl

hin: hin

Hinnom: HIN-uhm

hippodrome: HIP-uh-drohm

Hir: huhr

Hira: HYE-ruh

Hiram: HYE-ruhm

Hircanus: heer-KAY-nuhs

Hirsemes: heer-SEE-mes

Hittite: HIT-ite

Hivite: HYE-vite

Hizki: HIZ-kye

Hizkiah: hiz-KYE-uh

Hizkijah: hiz-KYE-juh

Hoba: HOH-buh

Hobab: HOH-bab

Hobah: HOH-buh

Hod: hahd

Hodaiah: hoh-DAY-uh

Hodaviah: HOH-duh-**VYE**-uh

Hodes: HOH-des

Hodesh: HOH-desh

Hodevah: hoh-DEE-vuh

Hodiah: hoh-DYE-uh

Hodijah: hoh-DYE-juh

Hodshi: HAHD-shye

Hodsi: HOD-sye

Hoglah: HOG-luh

Hoham: HOH-ham

Holda: HOHL-duh

Holofernes: HOL-uh-**FUHR**-neez

Holon: HOH-lahn

Holy Ghost: HOH-lee-gohst

Holy Spirit: HOH-lee-SPEER-it

Homam: HOH-mam

Homer: HOH-muhr

Hon: hahn

hoopoe: HOO-poo

Hophni: HOF-nye

Hophra: HOF-ruh

Hor: hor

Horam: HOR-am

Horeb: HOR-eb

Horem: HOR-em

Horesh: HOR-esh

Hor Haggidgad: HOR-huh-**GID**-gad

Hor-haggidgad: HOR-huh-**GID**-gad

Horhaggidgad: HOR-huh-**GID**-gad

Hor Hagidgad: HOR-huh-**GID**-gad

Hor-hagidgad: HOR-huh-**GID**-gad

Hori: HOR-eye

Horim: HOR-im

Horite: HOR-ite

Horma: HOR-muh

Horon: HOR-on

Horonaim: HOR-uh-**NAY**-im

Horonite: HOR-uh-nite

Horrhite: HOR-ite

Hosa: HOH-suh

Hosah: HOH-suh

hosanna: hoh-ZAN-uh

Hosea: hoh-ZAY-uh

Hoshaiah: hoh-SHAY-uh

Hoshama: HOSH-uh-muh

Hoshea: hoh-SHEE-uh

Hospitalis: HAHS-puh-**TAL**-is

Hotham: HOH-thuhm

Hothan: HO-thuhn

Hothir: HOH-thuhr

Hozai: HOH-zye

Hozeh: HOH-zeh

Hubbah: HUH-buh

Hucac: HUH-kahk

Hucuca: HUH-kah-kuh

Huddai: HUH-dye

Hukkok: HUH-kahk

Hukok: HEW-kahk

Hul: huhl

Huldah: HUHL-duh

Humtah: HUHM-tuh

Hupham: HEW-fuhm

Huphamite: HEW-fuh-mite

Huppah: HUP-uh

Huppim: HUP-him

Huppite: HUP-ite

Hur: huhr

Hurai: HEW-rye

Huram: HEW-ruhm

Huram-abi: HEW-ruhm-**AY**-bye

Huramabi: HEW-ruhm-**AY**-bye

Huri: HEW-rye

Hus: huhs

Husam: HEW-sam

Husathi: HEW-suh-thye

Husathite: HEW-suh-thite

Husati: HEW-suh-tye

Husha: HEW-shuh

Hushah: HEW-shuh

Hushai: HEW-shye

Husham: HEW-shuhm

Hushathite: HEW-shuh-thite

Hushim: HEW-shim

Hushite: HEW-shite

Husi: HEW-sye

Husim: HEW-sim

Huz: huhz

Huzoth: HUH-zahth

Huzzab: HUH-zuhb

Hydaspes: hye-DAS-peez

Hymenaeus: HYE-muh-**NEE**-uhs

Hymeneus: HYE-muh-**NEE**-uhs

Hyrcanus: heer-KAY-nuhs

hyssop: HIS-uhp

I

Ibhar: IB-hahr

Ibleam: IB-lee-uhm

Ibneiah: in-NEE-uh

Ibnijah: ib-NYE-juh

Ibri: IB-rye

Ibsam: IB-sam

Ibzan: IB-zan

Icamia: IK-uh-**MYE**-uh

I-chabod: I-kuh-bod

Ichabod: IK-uh-bod

Iconium: eye-KOH-nee-uhm

Icuthiel: i-KEW-thee-uhl

Idaia: i-DYE-uh

Idaias: i-DYE-uhs

Idalah: ID-uh-luh

Idbash: ID-bash

Iddo: ID-oh

Idida: i-DYE-duh

Idithum: i-DYE-thum

Idithun: i-DYE-thun

Idumaea: ID-yoo-**MEE**-uh

Idumaean: ID-yoo-**MEE**-uhn

Idumea: ID-yoo-**MEE**-uh

Idumean: ID-yoo-**MEE**-uhn

Iezer: eye-EE-zuhr

Iezerite: eye-EE-zuh-rite

Igal: EYE-gal

Igaal: EYE-gal

Igdaliah: IG-duh-**LYE**-uh

Igeal: EYE-gee-uhl

Ihelom: EYE-huh-lahm

Iim: EYE-im

Iishvah: eye-ISH-vuh

Ije Abarim: EYE-juh-**AB**-uh-rim

Ije-abarim: EYE-juh-**AB**-uh-rim

Ijeabarim: EYE-juh-**AB**-uh-rim

Ijim: EYE-jim

Ijon: EYE-jon

Ikkesh: IK-esh

Ilai: EYE-lye

Iliadun: i-LYE-uh-duhn

Illel: ILL-uhl

Illyria: i-LEER-ee-uh

Illyricum: i-LEER-eh-kuhm

Imalkue: i-MAL-kew-ee

Imla: IM-luh

Imlah: IM-luh

Immanuel: i-MAN-yoo-uhl

Immer: IM-uhr

Immite: IM-ite

Imna: IM-nuh

Imnah: IM-nuh

Imnahite: IM-nuh-hite

Imnite: IM-nite

Imrah: IM-ruh

Imri: IM-rye

India: IN-dee-uh

Indian: IN-dee-uhn

Iob: EYE-ohb

Ionian: eye-OH-nee-uhn

Itoa: eye-OH-tuh

Iphdeiah: if-**DEE**-uh

Iphedeiah: IF-uh-**DEE**-uh

Iphtah: IF-tuh

Iphtah El: **IF**-tuh-EL

Iphtah-el: **IF**-tuh-EL

Iphtahel: **IF**-tuh-EL

Ir: eer

Ira: EYE-ruh

Irad: EYE-rad

Iram: EYE-ram

Ir-hamelah: eer-HAM-uh-luh

Iri: EYE-rye

Irijah: eye-RYE-juh

Ir-Moab: eer-MOH-ab

Ir Nahash: eer-NAY-hash

Ir-nahash: eer-NAY-hash

Irnahash: eer-NAY-hash

Iron: EER-uhn

Irpeel: EER-pee-uhl

Ir Shemesh: eer-SHEM-ish

Ir-shemesh: eer-SHEM-ish

Irshemesh: eer-SHEM-ish

Iru: EYE-roo

Isaac: EYE-zuhk

Isaar: IS-har

Isai: EYE-zye

Isaiah: eye-ZAY-uh

Isaias: eye-ZAY-uhs

Isboseth: is-BOH-seth

Iscah: IS-kuh

Iscariot: is-KAIR-ee-uht

Isdael: IZ-dee-uhl

Ish: ish

Ishbaal: ISH-bay-uhl

Ishbah: ISH-buh

Ishbak: ISH-bak

Ishbi-benob: ISH-bye-**BEE**-nahb

Ishbibenob: ISH-bye-**BEE**-nahb

Ish-bosheth: ish-BOH-sheth

Ishbosheth: ish-BOH-sheth

Ish-hai: ISH-hye

Ishi: ISH-eye

Ishiah: i-SHYE-uh

Ishijah: i-SHYE-juh

Ishhod: ISH-hahd

Ishma: ISH-muh

Ishmael: ISH-may-uhl

Ishmaelite: ISH-may-uh-lite

Ishmaiah: ish-MAY-uh

Ishmeelite: ISH-mee-uhl-lite

Ishmerai: ISH-muh-rye

Ismiel: is-MEE-uhl

Ishpah: ISH-puh

Ishpan: ISH-pan

Ish-tob: ISH-tahb

Ishuai: ISH-yoo-eye

Ishui: ISH-yoo-eye

Ishvah: ISH-vuh

Ishvi: ISH-vye

Ishvite: IS-muh-**KYE**-uh

Ismael: IS-may-el

Ismaelite: IS-may-uhl-ite

Ismahel: IS-may-hel

Ismaiah: is-MYE-uh

Ismakiah: IS-muh-**KYE**-uh

Ispa: IS-puh

Ispah: IS-puh

Israel: IZ-ray-uhl

Israelite: IZ-ray-uh-lite

Israelitish: **IZ**-ray-uh-LITE-ish

Issachar: **IS**-uh-kahr

Issacharite: IS-uh-kuh-rite

Isshiah: i-SHYE-uh

Isshijah: i-SHYE-juh

Istalcurus: IS-tuhl-**KEWR**-uhs

Istemo: IS-tuh-moh

Istob: IS-tahb

Isuah: IS-yoo-uh

Isuhaia: IS-uh-**HYE**-uh

Isui: IS-yoo-eye

Italian: i-TAL-yuhn

Italica: i-TAL-eh-kuh

Italy: IT-uh-lee

Ithai: ITH-eye

Ithamar: ITH-uh-mar

Ithiel: ITH-ee-uhl

Ithlah: ITH-luh

Ithmah: ITH-muh

Ithnan: ITH-nan

Ithra: ITH-ruh

Ithran: ITH-ran

Ithream: ITH-ree-uhm

Ithrite: ITH-rite

Ittah-kazin: IT-uh-**KAY**-zin

Ittai: IT-eye

Ituraea: IT-yoor-**EE**-uh

Iturea: IT-yoor-**EE**-uh

Iturean: IT-yoor-**EE**-uhn

Ivvah: IV-uh

Iye Abarim: EYE-uh-**AB**-uh-rim

Iye-abarim: EYE-uh-**AB**-uh-rim

Iyeabarim: EYE-uh-**AB**-uh-rim

Iyim: EYE-yim

Iyyob: EYE-yahb

Izar: EYE-zahr

Izarahiah: IZ-uh-ruh-**HYE**-uh

Izehar: IZ-uh-hahr

Izeharite: IZ-uh-hahr-ite

Izhar: IZ-hahr

Izharite: IZ-huh-rite

Izliah: iz-LYE-uh

Izohar: eh-ZOH-hahr

Izrahia: IZ-ruh-**HYE**-uh

Izrahiah: IZ-ruh-**HYE**-uh

Izrahite: IZ-ruh-hite

Izri: IZ-rye

Izziah: i-ZYE-uh

J

Jaakan: JAY-uh-kan

Jaakanite: jay-A-kuh-nite

Jaakobah: jay-uh-KOH-buh

Jaakobath: jay-uh-KOH-bath

Jaala: JAY-uh-luh

Jaalah: JAY-uh-luh

Jaalam: JAY-uh-lam

Jaan: JAY-an

Jaanai: JAY-uh-nye

Jaar: JAY-uhr

Jaare-Oregim: JAY-uh-ree-**OR**-uh-gim

Jaareoregim: JAY-uh-ree-**OR**-uh-gim

Jaareshiah: JAY-uh-ree-**SHYE**-uh

Jaasai: JAY-uh-sye

Jaasau: JAY-uh-saw

Jaasiel: jay-AZ-ee-uhl

Jaasu: JAY-uh-soo

Jaazaniah: jay-AZ-uh-**NYE**-uh

Jaazer: JAY-uh-zuhr

Jaaziah: JAY-uh-**ZYE**-uh

Jaaziel: jay-AZ-ee-uhl

Jabal: JAY-buhl

Jabbok: JAB-uhk

Jabes: JAY-bez

Jabesh: JAY-besh

Jabesh Gilead: JAY-besh-**GIL**-ee-uhd

Jabesh-gilead: JAY-besh-**GIL**-ee-uhd

Jabez: JAY-bez

Jabin: JAY-bin

Jabneel: JAB-nee-uhl

Jabneh: JAB-neh

Jaboc: JAB-uhk

Jacan: JAY-kuhn

Jachan: JAY-kuhn

Jachanan: JAY-kuh-nuhn

Jachim: JAY-kim

Jachin: JAY-kin

Jachinite: JAY-kuh-nite

Jacim: JAY-kim

jacinth: JAY-sinth

Jacob: JAY-kuhb

Jacoba: juh-KOH-buh

Jacubus: juh-KEW-buhs

Jada: JAY-duh

Jadah: JAY-duh

Jadau: JAY-daw

Jaddai: JAD-eye

Jaddua: JAD-yoo-uh

Jaddus: JAD-uhs

Jadihel: juh-DYE-hel

Jadon: JAY-dahn

Jael: JAY-uhl

Jagur: JAY-guhr

Jah: jah

Jahaddai: juh-HAHD-dye

Jahaleleel: JAY-huh-**LEL**-ee-uhl

Jahath: JAY-hath

Jahaz: JAY-haz

Jahaza: juh-HAY-zuh

Jahazah: juh-HAY-zuh

Jahaziah: JAY-huh-**ZYE**-uh

Jahaziel: juh-HAY-zee-uhl

Jahdai: JAH-dye

Jahdiel: JAH-dee-uhl

Jahdo: JAH-doh

Jahel: JAY-huhl

Jahiel: juh-HYE-uhl

Jahleel: JAH-lee-uhl

Jahleelite: JAH-lee-uh-lite

Jahmai: JAH-mye

Jahzah: JAH-zuh

Jahzeel: JAH-zee-uhl

Jahzeelite: JAH-zee-uh-lite

Jahzeiah: jah-ZEE-uh

Jahzerah: JAH-zuh-ruh

Jahziel: JAH-zee-uhl

Jair: JAY-uhr

Jairite: JAY-uh-rite

Jairus: JYE-ruhs or jay-EYE-ruhs

Jakan: JAY-kuhn

Jakeh: JAY-kuh

Jakim: JAY-kim

Jakin: JAY-kin

Jakinite: JAY-kuh-nite

Jalam: JAY-luhm

Jalel: JAY-lel

Jaleleel: jay-LEL-lee-uhl

Jalelite: JAH-lee-lite

Jalon: JAY-lahn

Jambres: JAM-briz

Jambri: JAM-brye

James: jaymz

Jamin: JAY-min

Jaminite: JAY-meh-nite

Jamlech: JAM-lek

Jamnia: JAM-nee-uh

Jamnian: JAM-nee-uhn

Jamnite: JAM-nite

Jamra: JAM-ruh

Janai: JAY-nye

Janim: JAY-nim

Janna: JAN-uh

Jannai: JAN-eye

Jannes: JAN-iz

Janoah: juh-NOH-uh

Janoe: juh-NOH-uh

Janohah: juh-NOH-huh

Janum: JAY-nuhm

Japheth: JAY-feth

Japhia: juh-FYE-uh

Japhie: jah-FYE-uh

Japhlet: JAF-lit

Japhleti: JAF-luh-tye

Japhletite: JAF-luh-tite

Japho: JAY-foh

Jara: JAIR-uh

Jaramoth: JAIR-uh-mahth

Jare: JAIR-uh

Jareb: JAIR-eb

Jared: JAIR-ed

Jarephel: JAIR-uh-fel

Jaresiah: JAIR-uh-**SYE**-uh

Jarha: JAHR-huh

Jarib: JAIR-ib

Jarim: JAIR-im

Jarimoth: JAIR-uh-mahth

Jarkon: JAHR-kon

Jarmuth: JAHR-muhth

Jaroah: juh-ROH-uh

Jasa: JAZ-uh

Jasael: JAY-say-uhl

Jaser: JAY-zuhr

Jashar: JAY-shuhr

Jashen: JAY-shuhn

Jasher: JAY-shuhr

Jashobeam: juh-SHOH-bee-uhm

Jashub: JAY-shuhb

Jashubi: juh-SHOO-bye

Jashubi Lehem: juh-SHOO-bye-**LEE**-hem

Jashubi-lehem: juh-SHOO-bye-**LEE**-hem

Jashubite: JAY-shuh-bite

Jasiel: JAY-see-uhl

Jason: JAY-suhn

Jassa: JAZ-uh

Jassen: JAY-suhn

Jasub: JAY-soob

Jasubus: juh-SOO-buhs

Jatal: JAY-tuhl

Jathan: JAY-thuhn

Jathniel: JATH-nee-uhl

Jattir: JAT-uhr

Javan: JAY-vuhn

Jazer: JAY-zuhr

Jaziel: JAY-zee-uhl

Jaziz: JAY-ziz

Jeabarim: jay-AB-uh-rim

Jearim: JEE-uh-rim

Jeaterai: jee-AT-uh-rye

Jeatherai: jeh-ATH-uh-rye

Jebaar: JEB-hahr

Jebahar: JEB-uh-hahr

Jebania: JEB-uh-**NYE**-uh

Jeberechiah: jeh-BAIR-uh-**KYE**-uh

Jeberekiah: jeh-BAIR-uh-**KYE**-uh

Jeblaam: JEB-lay-uhm

Jebnael: JEB-nay-uhl

Jebneel: JEB-nay-uhl

Jeboc: JEB-uhk

Jebsem: JEB-sem

Jebus: JEE-buhs

Jebusi: JEB-yoo-sye

Jebusite: JEB-yoo-site

Jecamiah: JEK-uh-**MYE**-uh

Jecemia: JEK-uh-**MYE**-uh

Jechelia: JEK-uh-**LYE**-uh

Jechiliah: JEK-uh-**LYE**-uh

Jecholiah: JEK-uh-**LYE**-uh

Jechoniah: JEK-uh-**NYE**-uh

Jechonias: JEK-uh-**NYE**-uhs

Jecmaan: JEK-may-an

Jecnam: JEK-nuhm

Jecoliah: JEK-uh-**LYE**-uh

Jeconiah: JEK-uh-**NYE**-uh

Jeconias: JEK-uh-**NYE**-uhs

Jeconam: JEK-uh-nuhm

Jecsan: JEK-sahn

Jectan: JEK-tahn

Jectehel: JEK-tuh-hel

Jecthel: JEK-thuhl

Jedaia: jeh-DAY-uh

Jedaiah: jeh-DAY-uh

Jedala: JED-uh-luh

Jeddo: JED-doh

Jeddu: JED-oo

Jedebos: JED-uh-bahs

Jedeus: JED-ee-uhs

Jediael: jeh-DYE-ay-uhl

Jedidah: jeh-DYE-duh

Jedidiah: JED-uh-**DYE**-uh

Jediel: jeh-DYE-uhl

Jedihel: jeh-DYE-hel

Jeduthun: jeh-DEW-thuhn

Jeeli: JEE-uh-lye

Jeelus: jeh-EE-luhs

Jeezer: jeh-EE-zuhr

Jeezerite: jeh-EE-auh-rite

Jegar Sahadutha: JEE-guhr-say-huh-**DOO**-thuh

Jegar-sahadutha: JEE-guhr-say-huh-**DOO**-thuh

Jegarsahadutha: JEE-guhr-say-huh-**DOO**-thuh

Jehaleleel: JEE-huh-**LEE**-lee-uhl

Jehalelel: jeh-HAL-uh-luhl

Jehallel: juh-HAL-lel

Jehallelel: jeh-HAL-uh-lel

Jehath: JEE-hath

Jehaziel: jeh-HAZ-ee-uhl

Jehdeiah: jeh-DEE-uh

Jehezekel: jeh-HEZ-uh-kel

Jeheziel: jeh-HAY-zee-uhl

Jehezkel: jeh-HEZ-kel

Jehiah: jeh-HYE-uh

Jehias: jeh-HYE-uhs

Jehiel: jeh-HYE-uhl

Jehieli: jeh-HYE-uh-lye

Jehielite: jeh-HYE-uh-lite

Jehizkiah: JEE-hiz-**KYE**-uh

Jehoadah: jeh-HOH-uh-duh

Jehoaddah: jeh-HOH-uh-duh

Jehoaddan: jeh-HOH-uh-duhn

Jehoaddin: jeh-HOH-uh-din

Jehoahaz: jeh-HOH-uh-haz

Jehoash: jeh-HOH-ash

Jehohanan: JEE-hoh-**HAY**-nuhn

Jehoiachin: jeh-HOI-uh-kin

Jehoiada: jeh-HOI-uh-duh

Jehoiakim: jeh-HOI-uh-kim

Jehoiarib: jeh-HOI-uh-rib

Jehonadab: jeh-HOH-nuh-dab

Jehonathan: jeh-HON-uh-thuhn

Jehoram: jeh-HOR-uhm

Jehoshabeath: JEE-hoh-**SHAB**-ee-ath

Jehoshaphat: jeh-HOSH-uh-fat

Jehosheba: jeh-HOSH-uh-buh

Jehoshua: jeh-HOSH-yoo-uh

Jehoshuah: jeh-HOSH-yoo-uh

Jehovah: jeh-HOH-vuh

Jehovah-jireh: jeh-HOH-vuh-JYE-ruh

Jehovah-nissi: jeh-HOH-vuh-NIS-eye

Jehovah-shalom: jeh-HOH-vuh-**SHAH**-lohm

Jehozabad: jeh-HOH-zuh-bad

Jehozadak: jeh-HOH-zuh-dak

Jehu: JEE-hew

Jehubbah: jeh-HUB-uh

Jehucal: jeh-HEW-kuhl

Jehud: JEE-huhd

Jehudi: jeh-HEW-dye

Jehudijah: JEE-huh-**DYE**-juh

Jehuel: jeh-HEW-uhl

Jehukal: jeh-HEW-kuhl

Jehus: JEE-huhs

Jehush: JEE-huhsh

Jegaal: JEE-gahl

Jegbaa: JAG-bay-uh

Jegedelias: JAG-duh-**LYE**-uhs

Jeiel: jeh-EYE-uhl

Jekabzeel: jeh-KAB-zee-uhl

Jekameam: JEK-uh-**MEE**-uhm

Jekamiah: JEK-uh-**MYE**-uh

Jekoliah: JEK-uh-**LYE**-uh

Jekuthiel: jeh-KEW-thee-uhl

Jemai: JAH-mye

Jemima: jeh-MYE-muh

Jemimah: jeh-MYE-muh

Jeminah: jeh-MYE-nuh

Jemini: JEM-uh-nye

Jemla: JEM-luh

Jemlech: JEM-lek

Jemna: JEM-nah

Jemnaan: JEM-nay-uhn

Jemuel: JEM-yoo-uhl

Jenual: JEN-yoo-uhl

Jephdaia: jef-DYE-uh

Jephlat: JEF-lat

Jephleti: JEF-leh-tye

Jephone: jeh-FOO-nuh

Jephtahel: JEF-tuh-hel

Jephte: JEF-tee

Jephtha: JEF-thuh

Jephthae: JEF-thee

Jephthael: JEF-thee-uhl

Jephthah: JEF-thuh

Jephunneh: jeh-FUHN-nuh

Jeraa: JEER-uh

Jerah: JEER-uh

Jerahmeel: jeh-RAH-mee-uhl

Jerahmeelite: jeh-RAH-mee-uh-lite

Jerameel: jeh-RAH-mee-uhl

Jercaam: JAHR-kay-uhm

Jerechus: JAIR-uh-kuhs

Jered: JEER-ehd

Jeremai: JAIR-uh-mye

Jeremia: JAIR-eh-**MYE**-uh

Jeremiah: JAIR-eh-**MYE**-uh

Jeremias: JAIR-eh-**MYE**-uhs

Jeremiel: jeh-REM-ee-uhl

Jeremoth: JAIR-uh-mahth

Jeremy: JAIR-uh-mee

Jerenias: JAIR-uh-**NYE**-uhs

Jeriah: jeh-RYE-uh

Jerias: jeh-RYE-uhs

Jeribai: JAIR-uh-bye

Jericho: JAIR-uh-koh

Jeriel: JEER-eye-uhl

Jerijah: jeh-RYE-juh

Jerimoth: JAIR-uh-mahth

Jerimuth: JAIR-eh-muhth

Jerioth: JAIR-ee-ahth

Jerobaal: JAIR-uh-**BAY**-uhl

Jeroboam: jair-uh-**BOH**-uhm

Jeroham: je-ROH-huhm

Jeron: JAIR-uhn

Jersia: jair-SYE-uh

Jerub-baal: JAIR-ruhb-**BAY**-uhl

Jerubbaal: JAIR-ruhb-**BAY**-uhl

Jerub besheth: jeh-RUHB-uh-sheth

Jerub-besheth: jeh-RUHB-uh-sheth

Jerubbesheth: jeh-RUHB-uh-sheth

Jeruel: jeh-ROO-uhl

Jerusa: jeh-ROO-suh

Jerusah: jeh-ROO-suh

Jerusalem: jeh-ROO-suh-luhm

Jerusha: jeh-ROO-shah

Jerushah: jeh-ROO-shah

Jesaar: JES-uh-ahr

Jesaarite: jeh-SAHR-uh-rite

Jesaiah: jeh-SAY-uh

Jesamari: JES-uh-**MAHR**-eye

Jesarelah: JES-uh-**REE**-luh

Jesba: JES-buh

Jesbaam: JES-bay-uhm

Jesbaham: JES-bay-ham

Jesbibenob: JES-bye-**BEE**-nahb

Jesboc: JES-bahk

Jeseias: jeh-SAY-uhs

Jesema: JES-uh-muh

Jeser: JEE-zuhr

Jeshaiah: jeh-SHAY-uh

Jeshanah: JESH-uh-nuh

Jesharelah: JESH-uh-**REE**-luh

Jeshebeab: jeh-SHEB-ee-ab

Jesher: JESH-uhr

Jeshimon: jeh-SHYE-mahn

Jeshimoth: jeh-SHYE-mahth

Jeshishai: jeh-SHISH-eye

Jeshohaiah: JESH-uh-**HAY**-uh or JESH-uh-**HYE**-uh

Jeshoshaphat: jeh-SHOSH-uh-fat

Jeshua: JESH-yoo-uh

Jeshurun: JESH-uh-ruhn

Jeshush: JESH-ush

Jesi: JES-eye

Jesia: jeh-SYE-uh

Jesiah: jeh-SYE-uh

Jesiel: JES-ee-uhl

Jesimiel: jeh-SIM-ee-uhl

Jesimon: jeh-SYE-muhn

Jesimoth: jeh-SYE-mahth

Jesisi: jeh-SYE-sye

Jespha: JES-fuh

Jespham: JES-fam

Jesse: JES-ee

Jesshiah: jeh-SHYE-uh

Jessue: JESH-yoo-ee

Jessui: JESH-yoo-eye

Jesu: JEH-soo

Jesua JES-yoo-uh

Jesui: JES-yoo-eye

Jesuite: JES-yoo-ite

Jesurun: JES-uh-ruhn

Jesus: JEE-zuhs

Jesus ben-sira: JEE-zuhs-ben-**SYE**-ruh

Jesus ben-Sirach: JEE-zuhs-ben-**SYE**-ruhk

Jeta: JEH-tuh

Jeteba: JET-uh-buh

Jetebatha: JET-uh-**BAH**-thuh

Jeth: jeth

Jethela: JETH-uh-luh

Jether: JEE-thuhr

Jetherai: JETH-uh-rye

Jetheth: JEE-theth

Jethlah: JETH-luh

Jethma: JETH-muh

Jethnam: JETH-nam

Jethra: JETH-ruh

Jethraam: jeth-RAY-uhm

Jethrahem: jeth-RAY-hem

Jethrai: JETH-rye

Jethran: JETH-ruhn

Jethrite: JETH-rite

Jethro: JETH-roh

Jethson: JETH-suhn

Jetta: JET-uh

Jetur: JEE-tuhr

Jeuel: jeh-YOO-uhl

Jeush: JEE-ush

Jeuz: JEE-uhz

Jew: joo

Jewess: JOO-es

Jewish: JOO-ish

Jewry: JOO-ree

Jezabel: JEZ-uh-bel

Jezaniah: JEZ-uh-**NYE**-uh

Jezabad: JEZ-uh-bad

Jezebel: JEZ-uh-bel

Jezelus: JEZ-uh-luhs

Jezer: JEE-zuhr

Jezerite: JEE-zuh-rite

Jeziah: jeh-ZYE-uh

Jeziel: JEE-zee-uhl

Jezlia: jez-LYE-uh

Jezliah: jez-LYE-uh

Jezoar: jeh-ZOH-ahr

Jezonias: JEZ-uh-**NYE**-uhs

Jezra: JEZ-ruh

Jezrael: JEZ-ray-uhl

Jezrahel: JEZ-ruh-hel

Jezrahiah: JEZ-ruh-**HYE**-uh

Jezreel: JEZ-ree-uhl

Jezreelite: JEZ-ree-uh-lite

Jezreelitess: JEZ-ree-uh-lite-es

Jibsam: JIB-sam

Jidlaph: JID-laf

Jim: jim

Jimna: JIM-nuh

Jimnah: JIM-nuh

Jimnite: JIM-nite

Jiphtah: JIF-tuh

Jiphthah El: JIF-thuh-el

Jiphthah-el: JIF-thuh-el

Jiptah: JIP-tuh

Jishui: JISH-yoo-ee

Jisshiah: jeh-SHYE-uh

Jithra: JITH-ruh

Jithran: JITH-ruhn

Jizliah: jiz-LYE-uh

Jizri: JIZ-rye

Joab: JOH-ab

Joachaz: JOH-uh-kaz

Joachim: JOH-uh-kim

Joachin: JOH-uh-kin

Joada: joh-AD-uh

Joadan: joh-AD-uhn

Joadanus: joh-AD-uh-nuhs

Joah: JOH-uh

Joahaz: JOH-uh-haz

Joahe: JOH-uh-huh

Joakim: JOH-uh-kim

Joanan: joh-AY-nuhn

Joanna: joh-AN-uh

Joannan: joh-AN-uhn

Joannas: joh-AN-uhs

Joarib: JOH-uh-rib

Joas: JOH-as

Joash: JOH-ash

Joatham: JOH-uh-thuhm

Joathan: JOH-uh-thuhn

Joazabdus: JOH-uh-**ZAB**-duhs

Job: johb

Jobab: JOH-bab

Jobania: JOH-buh-**NYE**-uh

Jochanan: JOH-kuh-nuhn

Jochabed: JAHK-uh-bed

Jochebed: JAHK-uh-bed

jod: johd

Joda: JOH-duh

Jodan: JOH-duhn

Joed: JOH-ed

Joel: JOH-uhl

Joela: joh-EE-luh

Joelah: joh-EE-luh

Joezer: joh-EE-zuhr

Jogbehah: JAHG-buh-hah

Jogli: JAHG-lye

Joha: JOH-huh

Johanan: joh-HAY-nuhn

Johannan: joh-HAN-uhn

Johannes: joh-HAN-ehz

Johel: JOH-hel

John: jahn

Johojanan: JOH-hoh-**JAY**-nuhn

Joiada: JOI-uh-duh

Joiakim: JOI-uh-kim

Joiarib: JOI-uh-rib

Jokdeam: JAHK-dee-uhm

Jokim: JOH-kim

Jokmeam: JAHK-mee-uhm

Jokneam: JAHK-nee-uhm

Jokshan: JAHK-shan

Joktan: JAHK-tan

Joktheel: JAHK-thee-uhl

Jona: JOH-nuh

Jonadab: JOH-nuh-dab

Jonah: JOH-nuh

Jonam: JOH-nuhm

Jonan: JOH-nuhn

Jonas: JOH-nuhs

Jonathan: JAHN-uh-thuhn

Jonathas: JAHN-uh-thuhs

Jonath-elem-rechokim: JOH-nuhth-EE-luhm-ri-**KOH**-kim

Jonath Elem Rehoqim: JOH-nuhth-EE-luhm-ri-**HOH**-kim

Joppa: JOP-uh

Joppe: JOP-uh

Jorah: JOHR-uh

Jorai: JOHR-eye

Joram: JOHR-uhm

Jordan: JOHR-duhn

Joribas: juh-RYE-buhs

Joribus: juh-RYE-buhs

Jorim: JOHR-im

Jorkeam: JOHR-kee-uhm

Jorkoam: JOHR-koh-uhm

Josaba: JOH-suh-buh

Josabad: JOH-suh-bad

Josabhesed: JOH-sab-**HEE**-sehd

Josabia: JOH-suh-**BYE**-uh

Josachar: JOH-suh-kahr

Josaia: joh-SYE-uh

Josaphat: JAHS-uh-fat

Josaphias: JOH-suh-**FYE**-uhs

Jose: JOH-see

Josech: JOH-sehk

Josedec: JOH-suh-dek

Josedech: JOH-suh-dek

Joseph: JOH-suhf

Josephite: JOH-suh-fite

Josephus: joh-SEE-fuhs

Joses: JOH-siz

Joshah: JOH-shuh

Joshaphat: JAHSH-uh-fat

Joshaviah: JAHSH-uh-**VYE**-uh

Joshbekashah: JAHSH-beh-**KAY**-shuh

Josheb: JOH-shehb

Josheb-basshebeth: JOH-shehb-buh-**SHEE**-behth

Joshebbasshebeth: JOH-shehb-buh-**SHEE**-behth

Joshibiah: JAHSH-uh-**BYE**-uh

Joshua: JAHSH-yoo-uh

Josiah: joh-SYE-uh

Josias: joh-SYE-uhs

Josibiah: jahs-eh-BYE-uh

Josiphiah: jahs-eh-FYE-uh

Josue: jahs-OO-ee or JAHSH-yoo-uh

jot: jaht

Jota: JAH-tuh

Jotbah: JAHT-buh

Jotbath: JAHT-bath

Jotbathah: JOT-buh-thuh

Jotham: JOH-thuhm

Jozabad: JAH-zuh-bad

Jozacar: JOH-zuh-kahr

Jozachar: JOH-zuh-kahr

Jozadak: JOH-zuh-dak

Jubal: JOO-buhl

jubile: JOO-buh-lee

jubilee: JOO-buh-lee

Jucadam: JOO-kuh-dam

Jucal: JOO-kuhl

Juchal: JOO-kuhl

Jud: jood

Juda: JOO-duh

Judaea: joo-DEE-uh

Judaean: joo-DEE-uhn

Judah: JOO-duh

Judahite: JOO-duh-hite

Judaia: joo-DAY-uh

Judaism: JOO-duh-iz-uhm

Judas: JOO-duhs

Judas Iscariot: JOO-duhs-is-**KAIR**-ee-uht

Judas-Iscariot: JOO-duhs-is-**KAIR**-ee-uht

Jude: jood

Judea: joo-DEE-uh

Judean: joo-DEE-uhn

Judges: JUHJ-iz

Judi: JOO-dye

Judith: JOO-dith

Juel: JOO-uhl

Julia: JOO-lee-uh

Julius: JOO-lee-uhs

Junia: JOO-nee-uh

Junias: JOO-nee-uhs

Jupiter: JOO-puh-tuhr

Jushab Hesed: JOO-shab-**HEE**-sid

Jushab-hesed: JOO-shab-**HEE**-sid

Jushabhesed: JOO-shab-**HEE**-sid

Justus: JUHS-tuhs

Jutah: JOO-tuh

Juttah: JUT-uh

K

kab: kab

Kabzeel: KAB-zee-uhl

Kades: KAY-deez

Kadesh: KAY-dish

Kadesh Barnea: KAY-dish-**BAHR**-nee-uh

Kadesh-barnea: KAY-dish-**BAHR**-nee-uh

Kadeshbarnea: KAY-dish-**BAHR**-nee-uh

Kadesh-Meribah: KAY-dish-**MAIR**-uh-buh

Kadish: KAY-dish

Kadmeil: KAD-mee-uhl

Kadmonite: KAD-muh-nite

Kain: kayn

Kaiwan: KYE-wuhn

Kallai: KAL-eye

Kamon: KAY-muhn

Kanah: KAY-nuh

kaph: kaf

Kareah: kuh-REE-uh

Karim: KAIR-im

Karka: KAHR-kuh

Karkaa: KAHR-kay-uh

Karkor: KAHR-kor

Karmi: KAHR-mye

Karnaim: kahr-NAY-im

Karnion: KAHR-nee-uhn

Kartah: KAHR-tuh

Kartan: KAHR-tan

Kaserin: KAS-uh-rin

Kattah: KAT-uh

Katath: KAT-ath

Kebar: KEE-bahr

Kedar: KEE-duhr

Kegdarite: KED-uh-rite

Kedem: KEE-duhm

Kedemah: KED-uh-muh

Kedemite: KED-uh-mite

Kedemoth: KED-uh-moth

Kedesh: KEE-desh

Kedesh-naphtali: KEE-desh-**NAF**-tuh-lye

Kedorlaomer: KED-or-**LAY**-oh-muhr

Kedron: KEE-druhn

Kehelathah: KEE-huh-**LAY**-thuh

Keilah: kee-EYE-luh

Kelaiah: keh-LAY-uh

Kelal: KEE-lal

Kelita: keh-LYE-tuh

Kelub: KEE-luhb

Keluhi: KEL-yoo-hye

Kemuel: KEM-yoo-uhl

Kenaanah: keh-NAY-uh-nuh

Kenan: KEE-nuhn

Kenani: keh-NAY-nye

Kenaniah: KEN-uh-**NYE**-uh

Kenath: KEE-nath

Kenaz: KEE-naz

Kenez: KEE-nez

Kenezite: KEN-uh-zite

Kenezzite: KEN-uh-zite

Kenite: KEN-ite

Kenizzite: KEN-uh-zite

Kephar Ammoni: KEE-fuhr-**AM**-oh-nye

Kephar-ammoni: KEE-fuhr-**AM**-oh-nye

Kephira: keh-FYE-ruh

Kephirah: keh-FYE-ruh

Keran: KEE-ruhn

Keren-happuch: KAIR-uhn-**HAP**-uhk

Kerenhappuch: KAIR-uhn-**HAP**-uhk

Kerethite: KER-uh-thite

Kerioth: KAIR-ee-oth

Kerioth Hezron: KAIR-ee-oth-**HEZ**-ruhn

Kerioth-hezron: KAIR-ee-oth-**HEZ**-ruhn

Keriothhezron: KAIR-ee-oth-**HEZ**-ruhn

Kerith: KEER-ith

Keros: KEER-ahs

Kerub: KEER-uhb

Kesalon: KES-uh-luhn

Kesed: KEE-sid

Kesil: KEE-sil

Kesulloth: keh-SUHL-oth

Ketab: KEE-tab

Kethuvim: kuh-THOO-vim

Keturah: keh-TEW-ruh

Keveh: KEE-vuh

Kezia: keh-ZYE-uh

Keziah: keh-ZYE-uh

Kezib: KEE-zib

Keziz: KEE-ziz

Kibroth Hattaavah: KIB-rahth-huh-**TAY**-uh-vuh

Kibroth-hattaavah: KIB-rahth-huh-**TAY**-uh-vuh

Kibrothhattaavah: KIB-rahth-huh-**TAY**-uh-vuh

Kibzaim: kib-ZAY-im

Kidon: KYE-duhn

Kidron: KID-ruhn

Kilan: KYE-luhn

Kileab: KIL-ee-ab

Kilion: KIL-ee-uhn

Kilmad: KIL-mad

Kimham: KIM-ham

Kinah: KYE-nuh

King: king

Kinnereth: KIN-uh-reth

Kios: KYE-ahs

Kir: keer

Kir Haraseth: keer-**HAIR**-uh-seth

Kir-haraseth: keer-**HAIR**-uh-seth

Kir Hareseth: keer-**HAIR**-uh-seth

Kir-hareseth: keer-**HAIR**-uh-seth

Kirhareseth: keer-**HAIR**-uh-seth

Kir-haresh: keer-**HAIR**-ish

Kir heres: keer-**HEER**-iz

Kir-heres: keer-**HEER**-iz

Kirheres: keer-**HEER**-iz

Kiriath: **KEER**-ee-ath

Kiriathaim: **KEER**-ee-uh-**THAY**-im

Kiriath Arba: **KEER**-ee-ath-**AHR**-buh

Kiriath-arba: **KEER**-ee-ath-**AHR**-buh

Kiriatharba: **KEER**-ee-ath-**AHR**-buh

Kirath-arim: **KEER**-ee-ath-**AIR**-im

Kiratharim: **KEER**-ee-ath-**AIR**-im

Kiriath Baal: **KEER**-ee-ath-**BAY**-uhl

Kiriath-baal: **KEER**-ee-ath-**BAY**-uhl

Kiriathbaal: **KEER**-ee-ath-**BAY**-uhl

Kiriath Huzoth: **KEER**-ee-ath-**HEW**-zahth

Kiriath-huzoth: **KEER**-ee-ath-**HEW**-zahth

Kiriathhuzoth: **KEER**-ee-ath-**HEW**-zahth

Kiriathiarius: **KEER**-ee-ath-ee-**AIR**-ee-uhs

Kiriath Jearim: **KEER**-ee-ath-**JEE**-uh-rim

Kiriath-jearim: **KEER**-ee-ath-**JEE**-uh-rim

Kiriathjearim: **KEER**-ee-ath-**JEE**-uh-rim

Kiriath Sannah: **KEER**-ee-ath-**SAN**-uh

Kiriath-sannah: **KEER**-ee-ath-**SAN**-uh

Kiriathsannah: **KEER**-ee-ath-**SAN**-uh

Kiriath Sepher: **KEER**-ee-ath-**SEE**-fuhr

Kiriath-sepher: **KEER**-ee-ath-**SEE**-fuhr

Kiriathsepher: KEER-ee-ath-**SEE**-fuhr

Kirioth: KEER-ee-ahth

Kirjath: KEER-jath

Kirjathaim: KEER-juh-**THAY**-im

Kirjath Arba: KEER-jath-**AHR**-buh

Kirjath-arba: KEER-jath-**AHR**-buh

Kirjath Arim: KEER-jath-**AIR**-im

Kirjath-arim: KEER-jath-**AIR**-im

Kirjath Baal: KEER-jath-**BAY**-uhl

Kirjath-baal: KEER-jath-**BAY**-uhl

Kirjath Huzoth: KEER-jath-**HEW**-zahth

Kirjath-huzoth: KEER-jath-**HEW**-zahth

Kirjath Jearim: KEER-jath-**JEE**-uh-rim

Kirjath-jearim: KEER-jath-**JEE**-uh-rim

Kirjath Sannah: KEER-jath-**SAN**-uh

Kirjath-sannah: KEER-jath-**SAN**-uh

Kirjath Sepher: KEER-jath-**SEE**-fuhr

Kirjath-sepher: KEER-jath-**SEE**-fuhr

Kish: kish

Kishi: KISH-eye

Kishion: KISH-ee-uhn

Kishon: KYE-shahn

Kislev: KIS-lehv

Kislon: KIS-lahn

Kisloth Tabor: KIS-lahth-**TAY**-buhr

Kisloth-tabor: KIS-lahth-**TAY**-buhr

Kison: KEY-sahn

Kithlish: KITH-lish

Kitlish: KIT-lish

Kitron: KIT-rahn

Kittim: KIT-im

Kiyyun: KYE-uhn

knop: nahp

Koa: KOH-uh

Kohath: KOH-hath

Kohathite: KOH-huh-thite

Koheleth: koh-HEL-eth

Kola: KOH-luh

Kolaiah: koh-LAY-uh

Kona: KOH-nuh

koph: kohf

kor: kor

Korah: KOR-uh

Korahite: KOR-uh-hite

Korathite: KOR-uh-thite

Korazin: kor-AY-zin

Korban: KOR-ban

Kordan: KOR-dan

Kore: KOR-ee

Koreite: KOR-ee-ite

Korhite: KOR-hite

koum: koom

Koz: kahz

Kub: kuhb

Kue: KEW-ee

Kulom: KEW-luhm

kum: koom

Kun: koon

Kushaiah: koo-SHAY-uh

L

Laabim: LAY-uh-bim

Laad: LAY-had

Laada: LAY-uh-duh

Laadan: LAY-uh-dan

Laban: LAY-buhn

Labana: luh-BAY-nuh

Labanath: luh-BAY-nath

Labaoth: luh-BAY-ahth

Labo: LAY-boh

Laccunus: luh-KOO-nuhs

Lacedaemonian: LAS-uh-deh-**MOH**-nee-uhn

Lacedemon: luh-SID-eh-mohn

Lachis: LAY-kis

Lachish: LAY-kish

Lacunus: luh-KOO-nuhs

Ladan: LAY-duhn

Lael: LAY-uhl

Lahad: LAY-had

Lahai Roi: luh-HYE roi

Lahai-roi: luh-HYE roi

Lahela: la-HAY-luh

Lahem: LEE-hem

Lahmam: LAH-mam

Lahmas: LAH-mahs

Lahmi: LAH-mye

Lais: LAY-is

Laisa: LAY-i-suh

Laish: LAY-ish

Laishah: LAY-i-shah

Lakkum: LAK-uhm

Lakum: LAY-kuhm

lama: LAH-muh

Lamech: LAY-mehk

lamed: LAH-mid

lamedh: LAH-mid

Lamentation: LAM-en-**TAY**-shuhn

lamia: LAY-mee-uha

Lampsacus: lamp-SAY-cus

Lamuel: LEM-you-el

Laodicea: lay-OH-duh-**SEE**-uh

Laodicean: lay-OH-duh-**SEE**-uhn

Laomin: lay-UH-min

Lapidoth: LAP-eh-dahth

Lappidoth: LAP-eh-dahth

larus: LAHR-uhs

Lasaea: luh-SEE-uh

Lasea: luh-SEE-uh

Lasha: LAY-shuh

Lasharon: luh-SHAIR-uhn

Lasthenes: LAS-thuh-neez

Latin: LAT-in

Latussim: lat-YOO-sim

Lazarus: LAZ-uh-ruhs

Leah: LEE-uh

Leannoth: lee-AN-ahth

Lebana: leh-BAY-nuh

Lebanah: leh-BAY-nuh

Lebanon: LEB-uh-nuhn

Lebaoth: leh-BAY-ahth

Lebbaeus: leh-BEE-uhs

Lebbeus: leh-BEE-uhs

Leb Kamai: LEB kuh-**MYE**

Leb-kamai: LEB kuh-**MYE**

Lebna: LIB-nuh

Lebni: LIB-nye

Lebo Hamath: LEE-boh **HAY**-muhth

Lebo-hamath: LEE-boh **HAY**-muhth

Lebona: leh-BOH-nah

Lebonah: leh-BOH-nah

Lecah: LEE-kuh

Lecha: LEE-kuh

Lechi: LEE-kye

Leci: LEE-kye

Lecum: LEE-kuhm

Led: led

Legion: LEE-juhn

Lehab: LEE-hab

Lehabim: leh-HAY-bim

Lehabite: leh-HAY-byte

Lehem: LEE-hem

Leheman: leh-HAH-man

Lehi: LEE-hye

lema: luh-MAH

Lemuel: LEM-yoo-uhl

Lesa: LAY-suh

Lesem: LEE-shem

Leshem: LEE-shem

lethech: LEE-thik

lethek: LEE-thik

Lettus: LET-uhs

Letushim: leh-TOO-shim

Letushite: leh-TOO-shite

Leummim: lee-UH-mim

Leummite: lee-UH-mite

Leumonite: lee-OOM-uh-nite

Levi: LEE-vye

Leviathan: leh-VYE-uh-thuhn

Levis: LEE-vis

Levite: LEE-vite

Levitical: leh-VIT-eh-kuhl

Leviticus: leh-VIT-uh-kuhs

Lia: LEE-uh

Libanus: LEB-uh-nuhs

Libertine: LIB-uhr-teen

Libnah: LIB-nuh

Libnath: LIB-nath

Libni: LIB-nye

Libnite: LIB-nite

Libre Hayamim: LIB-reh-HAY-uh-mim

Libya: LIB-ee-uh

Libyan: LIB-ee-uhn

Lidebir: LID-uh-beer

Likhi: LIK-hye

Lilith: LIL-ith

Linus: LYE-nuhs

Lo-ammi: loh-AM-eye

Lobna: LAHB-nuh

Lobni: LAHB-nye

Lod: lahd

Lodabar: loh-DAY-buhr

Lo Debar: loh-DEE-buhr

Lo-debar: loh-DEE-buhr

Lodebar: loh-DEE-buhr

Lo Debar Karnaim: loh-DEE-buhr-kahr-**NAY**-im

Lois: LOH-is

Lord: lord

Lo-ruhama: LOH-roo-**HAH**-muh

Lo-ruhamah: LOH-roo-**HAH**-muh

Lot: laht

Lotan: LOH-tan

Lothasubus: loh-THAH-suh-buhs

Lozon: LOH-zahn

Lubim: LOO-bim

Lucas: LOO-kuhs

Lucifer: LOO-seh-fuhr

Lucius: LOO-shuhs

Lud: luhd

Ludim: LOO-dim

Ludite: LOO-dite

Luhith: LOO-hith

Luith: LOO-ith

Luke: look

Luz: luhz

Luza: luhz-uh

Lycaonia: LIK-uh-**OH**-nee-uh

Lycaonian: LIK-uh-**OH**-nee-uhn

Lycia: LISH-uh

Lydda: LID-uh

Lydia: LID-ee-uh

Lydian: LID-ee-uhn

Lysanias: leh-SAY-nee-uhs

Lysias: LIS-ee-uhs

Lysimachus: lye-SIM-uh-kuhs

Lystra: LIS-truh

M

Maacah: MAY-uh-kuh

Maacath: MAY-uh-kath

Maacathite: may-AK-uh-thite

Maacha: MAY-uh-kuh

Maachah: MAY-uh-kuh

Maachathi: may-AK-uh-thye

Maachathite: may-AK-uh-thite

Maadai: MAY-uh-dye

Maadiah: MAY-uh-**DYE**-uh

Maai: MAY-eye

Maakathite: may-AK-uh-thite

Maaleh-acrabbim: MAY-uh-leh-uh-**KRAB**-im

Maala: MAY-uh-luh

Maani: MAY-uh-nye

Maara: MAY-uh-ruh

Maarath: MAY-uh-rath

Maareh-geba: MAY-uh-reh-**GEE**-buh

Maasai: MAY-uh-sye

Maaseiah: MAY-uh-**SEE**-uh

Maasiai: may-AS-ee-eye

Maasias: may-AS-ee-uhs

Maasmas: may-AS-muhs

Maath: MAY-ath

Maaz: MAY-as

Maaziah: MAY-uh-**ZYE**-uh

Mabdai: MAB-dyd

Mabsam: MAB-sam

Mabsar: MAB-sahr

Macalon: muh-KAL-uhn

Macbannai: MAK-buh-nye

Macbenah: mak-BEE-nuh

Maccabee: MAK-uh-bee

Maccabeus: MAK-uh-**BEE**-uhs

Macces: MAY-kez

Maceda: muh-KEE-duh

Macedon: MAS-uh-dahn

Macedonia: MAS-uh-**DOH**-nee-uh

Macedonian: MAS-uh-**DOH**-nee-uhn

Macelloth: MAK-uh-lahth

Maceloth: MAK-uh-lahth

Macenias: MAK-uh-**NYE**-uhs

Macer: MAY-suhr

Machabee: MAK-uh-bee

Machabeus: MAK-uh-**BEE**-us

Machati: MAK-uh-tye

Machbanai: MAK-buh-nye

Machbani: MAK-buh-nye

Machbannai: mak-BAN-eye

Machbena: mak-BEE-nuh

Machbenah: mak-BEE-nuh

Machi: MAY-kye

Machir: MAY-keer

Machirite: MAY-kuh-rite

Machmas: MAK-muhs

Machmethath: MAK-muh-thath

Machnadebai: mak-NAD-uh-bye

Machpelah: mak-PEE-luh

Macnadebai: mak-NAD-uh-bye

Macron: MAY-krahn

Madaba: MAD-uh-buh

Madai: MAY-dye

Madan: MAY-dan

Madiabun: muh-DYE-uh-buhn

Madian: MAY-dee-uhn

Madmannah: mad-MAN-uh

Madmen: MAD-muhn

Madmena: mad-MEE-nuh

Madmenah: mad-MEE-nuh

Madon: MAY-dahn

Maelus: MAY-uh-luhs

Mag: mag

Magadan: MAG-uh-dan

Magala: MAG-uh-luh

Magbish: MAG-bish

Magdal: MAG-dahl

Magdala: MAG-duh-luh

Magdal-eder: MAG-duhl-**EE**-duhr

Magdalel: MAG-duhl-**EL**

Magdalen: MAG-duh-luhn

Magdalene: MAG-duh-leen

Magdalgad: MAG-duhl-**GAD**

Magdalum: MAG-duh-luhm

Magdiel: MAG-dee-uhl

Maged: MAY-gid

Mageddo: muh-GID-oh

Mageddon: muh-GID-uhn

Mageth: MAY-gath

Magi: MAY-jye

Magog: MAY-gog

Magor-missabib: MAY-gor-**MIS**-uh-bib

Magpiash: MAG-pee-ash

Magron: MAY-grahn

Magus: MAY-guhs

Mahalab: MAY-huh-lab

Mahalah: MAY-huh-lah

Mahalaleel: muh-HAY-luh-**LEE**-uhl

Mahalalel: muh-HAL-luh-luhl

Mahalath: MAY-huh-lath

Mahalath Leannoth: MAY-huh-lath-lee-**AN**-ahth

Mahalath-leannoth: MAY-huh-lath-lee-**AN**-ahth

Mahaleb: MAY-huh-leb

Mahali: MAH-huh-lye

Mahalon: MAY-huh-luhn

Mahanaim: MAY-huh-**NAY**-im

Mahanath: MAY-huh-nath

Mahaneh Dan: MAY-huh-nuh-**DAN**

Mahaneh-dan: MAY-huh-uh-**DAN**

Mahanehdan: MAY-huh-uh-**DAN**

Maharai: MAY-huh-rye

Mahath: MAY-hath

Mahavite: MAY-huh-vite

Mahazioth: muh-HAY-zee-ahth

Maheleth: MAY-uh-leth

Maher-shalal-hash-baz: MAY-huhr-SHAL-al-**HASH**-baz

Mahershalalhashbaz: MAY-huhr-SHAL-al-**HASH**-baz

Mahir: MAY-huhr

Mahlah: MAH-luh

Mahli: MAH-lye

Mahlite: MAH-lite

Mahlon: MAH-lahn

Mahol: MAY-hahl

Mahseiah: mah-SEE-uh

Mahumite: MAY-huh-mite

Maianeas: may-AN-ee-uhs

Makaz: MAY-kaz

Maked: MAY-kehd

Makheloth: mak-HEE-lahth

Maki: MAY-kye

Makir: MAY-keer

Makirite: MAY-kuh-rite

Makkedah: muh-KEE-duh

Maktesh: MAK-tesh

Malachi: MAL-uh-kye

Malachias: MAL-uh-**KYE**-uhs

Malachy: MAL-uh-kee

Malaleel: MAL-uh-**LEE**-uhl

Malasar: MAL-uh-zahr

Malcam: MAL-kam

Malcham: MAL-kam

Malchiah: mal-KYE-uh

Malchiel: MAL-kee-uhl

Malchielite: MAL-kee-uh-lite

Malchijah: mal-KYE-juh

Malchiram: mal-KYE-ruhm

Malchi-shua: MAL-kye-**SHOO**-uh

Malchishua: MAL-kye-**SHOO**-uh

Malchus: MAL-kuhs

Maleleel: muh-LEE-lee-uhl

Malkiel: MAL-kee-uhl

Malkielite: MAL-kee-uh-lite

Malkijah: mal-KYE-juh

Malkiram: mal-KYE-ruhm

Malki-Shua: MAL-kye-**SHOO**-uh

Malkishua: MAL-kye-**SHOO**-uh

Mallos: MAL-uhs

Mallothi: MAL-uh-thye

Malluch: MAL-uhk

Malluchi: MAL-uh-kye

Mallus: MAL-uhs

Malta: MAHL-tuh

Mamaias: muh-MAY-uhs

Mamdai: MAM-dye

mammon: MAM-uhn

Mamre: MAM-ree

Mamuchus: muh-MEW-kuhs

Manach: MAN-ak

Manaen: MAN-ee-uhn

Manahath: MAN-uh-hath

Manahathite: MAN-uh-**HUH**-thite

Manahem: MAN-uh-hem

Manahethite: MAN-uh-**HEH**-thite

Manaim: muh-NAY-im

Manasseas: muh-NAS-ee-uhs

Manasseh: muh-NAS-uh

Manassehite: muh-NAS-uh-hite

Manasses: muh-NAS-eez

Manassite: muh-NAS-ite

MANE: MAY-nee

maneh: MAY-neh

Mani: MAY-nye

Manilius: muh-NIL-ee-uhs

Manius: MAY-nee-uhs

Manlius: MAN-lee-uhs

Manna: MAN-uh

manna: man-uh

Manoah: muh-NOH-uh

Manoko: MAN-uh-koh

Manue: muh-NEW-uh

Manuhoth: muh-NEW-hahth

Maoch: MAY-ahk

Maon: MAY-ahn

Maonathi: may-AHN-uh-thye

Maonite: MAY-uh-nite

Maozim: MAY-uh-zeem

Mapsam: MAP-sam

Mara: MAIR-uh

Marah: MAIR-uh

Maraioth: meh-RAY-ahth

Maralah: MAHR-uh-luh

maran atha: MAIR-uh-**NATH**-uh or MAHR-uh-**NATH**-uh

maran-atha: MAIR-uh-**NATH**-uh or MAHR-uh-**NATH**-uh

maranatha: MAIR-uh-**NATH**-uh or MAHR-uh-**NATH**-uh

Marcaboth: MAHR-kuh-bahth

Marcus: MAHR-kuhs

Mardochai: MAHR-duh-kye

Mardocheus: MAHR-duh-**KEE**-uhs

Mardochias: MAHR-duh-**KYE**-uhs

Marduk: MAHR-dewk

Mareal: MAY-ree-uhl

Marealah: MAHR-uh-luh

Maresa: muh-REE-suh

Mareshah: muh-REE-shuh

Mareth: MAY-reth

Mariam: MAIR-ee-uhm

Marimoth: MAIR-eh-mahth

Marisa: MAHR-uh-suh

Mark: mahrk

Marma: MAHR-muh

Marmoth: MAHR-mahth

Maroth: MAIR-ahth

Mars: mahrz

Marsena: mahr-SEE-nuh

Martha: MAHR-thuh

Mary: MAIR-ee

Masal: MAH-suhl

Masaloth: MAS-uh-lahth

Maschil: MAS-kil

Masepha: MAZ-puh

Maserite: MAZ-uh-rite

Maserophot: MAZ-ro-fat

Mash: mash

Mashal: MAY-shuhl

Masiah: muh-SYE-uh

Masias: muh-SYE-uhs

Maskil: MAS-kil

Masma: MAS-muh

Masman: MAS-muhn

Masmana: mas-MAN-uh

Masobia: muh-ZO-bee-uh

Maspha: MAS-fuh

Masphath: MAS-fath

Masreca: MAS-ruh-kuh

Masrekah: MAS-ruh-kuh

Massa: MAS-uh

Massah: MAS-uh

Massaite: MAS-ay-ite

Masseiah: muh-SEE-uh

Massias: muh-SYE-uhs

Mathan: MATH-uhn

Mathana: MATH-uh-nuh

Mathania: MATH-uh-**NYE**-uh

Mathanias: MAT-uh-**NYE**-uhs

Mathanite: MATH-uh-nite

Mathathias: MATH-uh-**THYE**-uhs

Mathca: MATH-kuh

Mathusala: muh-THOO-suh-luh

Mathusale: muh-THOO-suh-luh

Matred: MAY-tred

Matri: MAY-trye

Matrite: MAY-trite

Mattan: MAT-uhn

Mattanah: MAT-uh-nuh

Mattaniah: MAT-uh-**NYE**-uh

Mattatha: MAT-uh-thuh

Mattathah: MAT-uh-thuh

Mattathiah: MAT-uh-**THYE**-uh

Mattathias: MAT-uh-**THYE**-uhs

Mattattah: MAT-uh-tuh

Mattenai: MAT-uh-nye

Matthan: MATH-an

Matthanias: MATH-uh-**NYE**-uhs

Matthat: MATH-at

Matthelas: MATH-uh-luhs

Matthew: MATH-yoo

Matthias: muh-THYE-uhs

Mattithiah: MAT-uh-**THYE**-uh

Maviael: MAH-vee-**AY**-el

Mazitias: MAZ-uh-**TYE**-uhs

Mazzaroth: MAZ-uh-rahth

Meah: MEE-uh

Meani: mee-AY-nye

Mearah: mee-AIR-uh

Mebunnai: meh-BUHN-eye

Mecherathite: meh-KAIR-uh-thite

Meconah: meh-KOH-nuh

Medaba: MED-uh-buh

Medad: MEE-dad

Medan: MEE-dan

Meddin: MED-din

Mede: meed

Medeba: MED-uh-buh

Medemena: MED-uh-**MEN**-uh

Media: MEE-dee-uh

Median: MEE-dee-uhn

Mediterranean: MED-i-tuh-**RAY**-nee-uhn

Meeda: meh-EE-duh

Meetabel: meh-HET-uh-bel

Megeddon: muh-GED-on

Megiddo: meh-GID-oh

Megiddon: meh-GID-on

Mehallalel: muh-HAL-uh-lel

Mehetabeel: meh-HET-uh-**BEE**-uhl

Mehetabel: meh-HET-uh-bel

Mehida: meh-HYE-duh

Mehir: MEE-huhr

Meholah: meh-HOH-luh

Meholathite: meh-HOH-luh-thite

Mehujael: meh-HEW-jay-uhl

Mehuman: meh-HEW-muhn

Mehunim: meh-HEW-nim

Mehusim: meh-HEW-sim

Mejarcon: meh-JAHR-kon

Me Jarkon: meh-JAHR-kon

Me-jarkon: meh-JAHR-kon

Mejarkon: meh-JAHR-kon

Mekerathite: meh-KER-uh-thite

Mekonah: meh-KOH-nuh

Melah: MEE-luh

Melakim: MEL-uh-kim

Melatiah: MEL-uh-**TYE**-uh

Melcha: MEL-kuh

Melchi: MEL-kye

Melchia: mel-KYE-uh

Melchiah: mel-KYE-uh

Melchias: mel-KYE-uhs

Melchiel: MEL-kee-uhl

Melchiram: mel-KYE-ruhm

Melchisedec: mel-KIS-uh-dek

Melchi-shua: MEL-kye-**SHOO**-uh

Melchishua: MEL-kye-**SHOO**-uh

Melchisua: MEL-kye-**SOO**-uh

Melchizedec: mel-KIZ-uh-dek

Melchom: MEL-kuhm

Melea: MEE-lee-uh

Melech: MEE-lek

Melichu: MEL-eh-kew

Melicu: MEL-eh-kew

Melita: MEL-eh-tuh

Melki: MEL-kye

Mello: MEL-oh

Meloch: MAL-uk

Melzar: MEL-zahr

mem: maym

Memmius: MEM-ee-uhs

Memphis: MEM-fis

Memucan: meh-MEW-kuhn

Menahem: MEN-uh-hem

Menan: MEE-nan

mene: MEE-nee

Menelaus: MEN-uh-**LAY**-uhs

Menestheus: meh-NES-thee-uhs

Meni: muh-NEE

Menna: MEN-uh

Menni: MEN-eye

Mennith: MEN-ith

Menuhoth: min-YOO-hoth

Menuim: MEN-yoo-im

Meon: MEE-on

Meonenim: mee-ON-uh-nim

Meonothai: mee-ON-oh-thye

Mephaath: meh-FAY-ath

Mephibosheth: meh-FIB-oh-sheth

Merab: MEE-rab

Meraiah: meh-RAY-uh

Meraioth: meh-RAY-ahth

Merala: MAR-eh-luh

Meran: MER-uhn

Merari: muh-RAY-rye or meh-RAH-rye

Merarite: muh-RAY-rite or meh-RAH-rite

Merathaim: MER-uh-**THAY**-im

Mercurius: muhr-KYOOR-ee-uhs

Mered: MEE-red

Meremoth: MER-uh-mahth

Meres: MEE-rez or MEE-reez

Meribah: MER-eh-bah

Meribah Kadesh: MER-eh-bah-**KAY**-dish

Meribah-kadesh: MER-eh-bah-**KAY**-dish

Meribath: MER-eh-bath

Meribath-kadesh: MER-eh-buhth-**KAY**-dish

Meribathkadesh: MER-eh-buhth-**KAY**-dish

Merib Baal: MER-ib-**BAY**-uhl

Merib-baal: MER-ib-**BAY**-uhl

Meribbaal: MER-ib-**BAY**-uhl

Meriboth: MER-eh-bahth

Merob: MEE-rahb

Merodach: meh-ROH-dak

Merodach Baladan: meh-ROH-dak-**BAL**-uh-duhn

Merodach-baladan: meh-ROH-dak-**BAL**-uh-duhn

Merodachbaladan: meh-ROH-dak-**BAL**-uh-duhn

Merom: MEE-rahm

Merome: MEE-rohm

Meron: MEE-rahn

Meronoth: meh-RAHN-ahth

Meronothite: meh-RAHN-oh-thite

Meroz: MEE-rahz

Merran: MER-uhn

Merrha: MER-hah

Meruth: MEE-ruhth

Mesa: MEE-suh

Mesaloth: MES-uh-lahth

Mesech: MEE-sehk

Mesha: MEE-shuh

Meshach: MEE-shak

Meshech: MEE-shek

Meshek: MEE-shek

Meshelemiah: meh-SHEL-uh-**MYE**-uh

Meshezabeel: meh-SHEZ-uh-bee-uhl

Meshezabel: meh-SHEZ-uh-bel

Meshillemith: meh-SHIL-uh-mith

Meshillemoth: meh-SHIL-uh-mahth

Meshobab: meh-SHOH-bab

Meshullam: meh-SHOOL-uhm

Meshullemeth: meh-SHOOL-uh-mith

Mesobaite: meh-SOH-bay-ite

Mesopotamia: MES-uh-puh-**TAY**-mee-uh

Mesphe: MIZ-pah

Mesrai: mez-RAY-eye

Mesraim: mez-RAY-im

Messa: MEE-suh

Messal: MEE-suhl

Messalemeth: meh-SHEL-uh-meth

Messiah: muh-SYE-uh

Messias: muh-SYE-uhs

Messulam: meh-SOOL-um

Meterus: muh-TEE-ruhs

Metheg Ammah: MEE-thig-**AM**-uh

Metheg-ammah: MEE-thig-**AM**-uh

Methegammah: MEE-thig-**AM**-uh

Methegh-ammah: MEE-thig-**AM**-uh

Methoar: meh-THOH-ahr

Methusael: meh-THOO-say-el

Methuselah: meh-THOO-suh-luh

Methushael: meh-THOO-shay-uhl

Metri: MEE-trye

Meunim: meh-YOO-nim

Meunite: meh-YOO-nite

Meza: MEE-zuh

Mezaab: MEE-zuh-ab

Me-zahab: MEE-zuh-hab

Mezahab: MEE-zuh-hab

Mezobaite: meh-ZOH-bay-ite

Mezobian: meh-ZOH-bee-uhn

Miamin: MYE-uh-min

Mibahar: MIB-uh-hahr

Mibhar: MIB-hahr

Mibsam: MIB-sam

Mibzar: MIB-zahr

Mica: MYE-kuh

Micah: MYE-kuh

Micaiah: mi-KAY-uh

Micha: MYE-kuh

Michael: MYE-kay-uhl or MYE-kuhl

Michah: MYE-kuh

Michaiah: mi-KAY-uh

Michal: MYE-kuhl

Michas: MYE-kuhs

Micheas: MIK-ee-uhs

Michmas: MIK-mas

Michmash: MIK-mash

Michmethah: MIK-muh-thuh

Michmethath: MIK-muh-thath

Michol: MYE-kuhl

Michri: MIK-rye

Michtam: MIK-tam

Micmash: MIK-mash

Micmethath: MIK-muh-thath

Micri: MIK-rye

Middin: MID-uhn

Midian: MID-ee-uhn

Midianite: MID-ee-uh-nite

Midianitish: MID-ee-uh-nite-ish

midrash: MID-rash

Migdal Eder: MIG-duhl-**EE**-duhr

Migdal-eder: MIG-duhl-**EE**-duhr

Migdal El: **MIG**-duhl-EL

Migdal-el: **MIG**-duhl-EL

Migdalel: **MIG**-duhl-EL

Migdal Gad: **MIG**-duhl-GAD

Migdal-gad: **MIG**-duhl-GAD

Migdalgad: **MIG**-duhl-GAD

Migdal-shechem: MIG-duhl-**SHEK**-uhm

Migdol: MIG-dahl

Migron: MIG-rahn

Mijamin: MIJ-uh-min

Mikloth: MIK-lahth

Mikneiah: mik-NEE-uh

Miktam: MIK-tam

Milalai: MIL-uh-lye

Milcah: MIL-kuh

Milcham: MIL-kam

Milcom: MIL-kuhm

Miletum: mye-LEE-tuhm

Miletus: mye-LEE-tuhs

Millo: MIL-oh

mina: MYE-nuh

Miniamin: MIN-yuh-min

Minjamin: MIN-juh-min

Minni: MIN-eye

Minnith: MIN-ith

Miphiboseth: meh-FIB-oh-seth

Miphkad: MIF-kad

Miriam: MEER-ee-uhm

Mirma: MEER-muh

Mirmah: MEER-muh

Misaam: MIS-ay-uhm

Misach: MIS-ak

Misael: MIS-ay-uhl

Misgab: MIS-gab

Mishael: MISH-ay-uhl

Mishal: MYE-shuhl

Misham: MYE-shuhm

Misheal: MISH-ee-uhl

Mishle: MISH-lee

Mishma: MISH-muh

Mishmannah: mish-MAN-uh

Mishpat: MISH-paht

Mishraite: MISH-ray-ite

Mispar: MIS-pahr

Mispereth: mis-PEE-rith

Misrephoth: MIS-ruh-fahth

Misrephoth Maim: MIS-ruh-fahth-**MAY**-im

Misrephoth-maim: MIS-ruh-fahth-**MAY**-im

Misrephothmaim: MIS-ruh-fahth-**MAY**-im

mite: mite

Mithan: MITH-uhn

Mithcah: MITH-kuh

Mithkah: MITH-kuh

Mithnite: MITH-nite

Mithredath: MITH-ruh-dath

Mithridates: MITH-ruh-**DAY**-teez

Mitylene: MIT-uh-**LEE**-nee

Mizar: MYE-zahr

Mizpah: MIZ-puh

Mizpah-gilead: MIZ-puh-**GIL**-ee-uhd

Mizpar: MIZ-pahr

Mizpeh: MIZ-peh

Mizraim: miz-RAY-im

Mizzah: MIZ-uh

mna: MYE-nuh

Mnason: NAY-suhn

Mnestheus: meh-NES-thee-uhs

Moab: MOH-ab

Moabite: MOH-uh-bite

Moabitish: MOH-uh-bite-ish

Moach: MOH-ahk

Moadiah: MOH-uh-**DYE**-uh

Mobonnai: muh-BOH-nye

Mochmur: MAHK-muhr

Mochori: MAHK-oh-rye

Modein: MOH-deen

Modin: MOH-din

Moeth: MOH-eth

Mohola: muh-HOH-lah

Moholi: muh-HOH-lye

Moholite: muh-HOH-ite

Molada: MOH-luh-duh

Moladah: MOH-luh-duh

Molathi: MOH-luh-thye

Molathite: MOH-luh-thite

Molchom: MOHL-kuhm

Molech: MOH-lek

Molecheth: moh-LEK-ith

Moli: MOH-lye

Molid: MOH-lid

Moloch: MOH-lahk

Momdis: MOM-dis

Momdius: MOM-dee-uhs

Moos: MOH-ahs

Moosias: MOH-uh-**SYE**-uhs

Moossias: MOH-uh-**SYE**-uhs

Morasthi: MOH-ruhs-tye

Morasthite: MOH-ruhs-thite

Morastite: MOH-ruhs-tite

Mordecai: MOHR-duh-kye

Moreh: MOHR-eh

Moresheth: MOHR-uh-sheth

Moresheth Gath: MOR-uh-sheth-**GATH**

Moresheth-gath: MOR-uh-sheth-**GATH**

Moreshethgath: MOR-uh-sheth-**GATH**

Moriah: muh-RYE-uh

Mosa: MOH-suh

Mosabab: MOH-suh-bab

Mosallam: moh-SAHL-uhm

Mosel: MOH-suhl

Mosera: moh-SEE-ruh

Moserah: moh-SEE-ruh

Moseroth: moh-SEE-ruhth

Moses: MOH-zehs

Mosoch: MOH-sahk

Mosollam: moh-SAHL-uhm

Mosollamia: moh-SAHL-uh-**MY**-uh

Mosollamith: moh-SAHL-uh-mith

Moza: MOH-zuh

Mozah: MOH-zuh

Muppim: MUH-pim

Musach: MEW-sak

Mushi: MEW-shye

Mushite: MEW-shite

Musi: MEW-sye

Musite: MEW-site

Musri: MEWS-rye

Muth Labben: mewth-LAB-uhn

Muth-labben: mewth-LAB-uhn

Myndos: MIN-dohs

Myndus: MIN-duhs

Myra: MYE-ruh

Mysia: MIS-ee-uh

Mysian: MIS-ee-uhn

N

Naalol: NAY-uh-lahl

Naam: NAY-uhm

Naamah: NAY-uh-muh

Naaman: NAY-uh-muhn

Naamanite: NAY-uh-muh-nite

Naamath: NAY-uh-muhth

Naamathite: NAY-uh-muh-thite

Naamite: NAY-uh-mite

Naara: NAY-uh-ruh

Naarah: NAY-uh-ruh

Naarai: NAY-uh-rye

Naaran: NAY-uh-ruhn

Naarath: NAY-uh-ruhth

Naaratha: NAY-uh-ruhth-uh

Naaria: NAY-uh-**RYE**-uh

Naas: NAY-as

Naashon: NAY-uh-shahn

Naasson: NAY-uh-sahn

Naathus: NAY-uh-thuhs

Nabal: NAY-buhl

Nabaioth: neh-BAY-ahth

Nabajoth: NAY-buh-jahth

Nabariah: NAB-uh-**RYE**-uh

Nabarias: NAB-uh-**RYE**-uhs

Nabat: NAY-bat

Nabatean: NAB-uh-**TEE**-uhn

Nabathite: NAB-uh-thite

Nabo: NAY-boh

Naboth: NAY-bahth

Nabuchodonosar: NAB-uh-kuh-**DAHN**-uh-sahr

Nabuchodonosor: NAB-uh-kuh-**DAHN**-uh-sohr

Nabuthean: NAB-uh-**THEE**-un

Nabuzardan: NAB-yoo-**ZAHR**-dan

Nachon: NAY-kahn

Nachor: NAY-kohr

Nacon: NAY-kahn

Nadab: NAY-dab

Nadabath: NAD-uh-bath

Nadabatha: nuh-DAB-uh-thuh

Nadabia: NAD-uh-**BYE**-uh

Nadib: NAY-dib

Naggae: NAG-ee

Naggai: NAG-eye

Nagge: NAG-ee

Nahabi: NAY-huh-bye

Nahalal: NAY-huh-lal

Nahale-gaash: NAY-huh-lee-**GAY**-ash

Nahaliel: nuh-HAY-lee-uhl

Nahallal: nuh-HAL-uhl

Nahalol: NAY-huh-lahl

Naham: NAY-ham

Nahamani: NAY-huh-**MAY**-nye

Naharai: NAY-huh-rye

Naharaim: NAY-huh-**RAY**-im

Nahari: NAY-huh-rye

Nahash: NAY-hash

Nahasson: NAY-huh-suhn

Nahath: NAY-hath

Nahbi: NAH-bye

Nahor: NAY-hor

Nahshon: NAH-shahn

Nahum: NAY-huhm

Naidus: NYE-duhs

Naim: naym

Nain: nayn

Naioth: NAY-ahth

Najoth: NAY-jahth

Namsi: NAM-sye

Namuel: NAM-yoo-el

Nanaea: nuh-NEE-uh

Nanaeon: nuh-NEE-uhn

Nanea: nuh-NEE-uh

Nangae: NAN-gee

Naomi: nay-OH-mee

Naphath: NAY-fath

Naphath-dor: NAY-fath-**DOHR**

Naphathdor: NAY-fath-**DOHR**

Napheg: NAY-feg

Napheth: NAY-fith

Naphis: NAY-fis

Naphish: NAY-fish

Naphisi: NAF-eh-sye

Naphoth: NAY-fahth

Naphoth Dor: NAY-foth-**DOHR**

Naphoth-dor: NAY-foth-**DOHR**

Naphothdor: NAY-foth-**DOHR**

Naphtali: NAF-tuh-lye

Naphtalite: NAF-tuh-lite

naphthar: NAF-thahr

Naphtuh: NAF-tuh

Naphtuhim: NAF-tuh-him

Naphtuhite: NAF-tuh-hite

Narcissus: nahr-SIS-uhs

Nasbas: NAS-buhs

Nashim: NAY-shim

Nasith: NAY-sith

Nasor: NAY-sohr

Nathan: NAY-thuhn

Nathanael: nuh-THAN-ay-uhl

Nathanel: nuh-THAN-uhl

Nathaniah: NATH-uh-**NYE**-uh

Nathanias: NATH-uh-**NYE**-uhs

Nathan-melech: NAY-thuhn-**MEE**-lehk

Nathanmelech: NAY-thuhn-**MEE**-lehk

Nathinean: NATH-uh-**NEE**-uhn

Naum: NAY-uhm

Nave: nayv

Nazarene: NAZ-uh-reen

Nazareth: NAZ-uh-rith

Nazarite: NAZ-uh-rite

Nazirite: NAZ-uh-rite

Nazorean: NAZ-uh-**REE**-uhn

Neah: NEE-uh

Neapolis: nee-AP-uh-lis

Neariah: NEE-uh-**RYE**-uh

Nebahaz: NEB-uh-haz

Nebai: NEE-bye

Nebaioth: neh-BAY-yahth

Nebajoth: neh-BAY-jahth

Neballat: neh-BAL-uht

Nebat: NEE-bat

Nebo: NEE-boh

Nebo-sarsekim: NEE-boh-**SAHR**-suh-kim

Nebsan: NIB-suhn

Nebuchadnezzar: NEB-uh-kuhd-**NEZ**-uhr

Nebuchadrezzar: NEB-uh-kuhd-**DREZ**-uhr

Nebushasban: NEB-uh-**SHAS**-ban

Nebushazban: NEB-uh-**SHAZ**-ban

Nebuzar-adan: NEB-uh-zahr-**AY**-duhn

Nebuzaradan: NEB-uh-zuh-**RAY**-duhn

Neceb: NEE-kehb

Nechao: neh-KAY-oh

Necho: NEE-koh

Nechoh: NEE-koh

Neco: NEE-koh

Necodan: neh-KOH-duhn

Nedabiah: NED-uh-**BYE**-uh

Neemias: NEE-uh-**MYE**-uhs

Negav: NEG-ev

Negeb: NEG-eb

Neginah: NEG-i-nuh

Neginoth: NEG-i-nahth

Nego: NEE-goh

Nehelam: neh-HEL-uhm

Nehelamite: neh-HEL-uh-mite

Nehelescol: neh-HEL-uhs-kahl

Nehemiah: NEE-huh-**MYE**-uh

Nehemias: NEE-huh-**MYE**-uhs

Nehemyah: neh-HEM-yuh

Nehiel: neh-HYE-uhl

Nehiloth: NEE-huh-lahth

Nehum: NEE-huhm

Nehushta: neh-HOOSH-tuh

Nehushtan: neh-HOOSH-tuhn

Neiel: neh-EYE-uhl

Nekeb: NEE-keb

Nekoda: neh-KOH-duh

Nemra: NEM-ruh

Nemrim: NIM-rim

Nemrod: NIM-rahd

Nemuel: NEM-yoo-uhl

Nemuelite: NEM-yoo-uh-lite

Nephath-Dor: NEE-fath-**DOHR**

Nepheg: NEE-fig

nephi: NEF-eye

Nephilim: NEF-uh-lim

Nephish: NEF-ish

Nephishesim: neh-FISH-uh-sim

Nephisim: neh-FYE-sim

Nephtali: NEF-tuh-lye

Nephthali: NEF-thuh-lye

Nephthalim: NEF-thuh-lim

Nephthar: NEF-thahr

Nephtoa: nef-TOH-uh

Nephtoah: nef-TOH-uh

Nephtuim: nef-TEW-im

Nephushesim: neh-FEW-shuh-sim

Nephusim: neh-FEW-sim

Nephusite: neh-FEW-site

Nephussim: neh-FEW-sim

Nepthalim: NEF-thuh-lim

Ner: nuhr

Neraiah: neh-RAY-uh

Neregel Sereser: NUHR-gal-suh-**REE**-zuhr

Nereus: NEE-rye-yoos

Nergal: NUHR-gal

Nergal-sar-ezer: NUHR-gal-suh-**REE**-zuhr

Nergal-sarezer: NUHR-gal-suh-**REE**-zuhr

Nergal-sharezer: NUHR-gal-shuh-**REE**-zuhr

Nergalsharezer: NUHR-gal-shuh-**REE**-zuhr

Nergel: NUHR-gal

Neri: NEE-rye

Neriah: neh-RYE-uh

Nerias: neh-RYE-uhs

Nero: NEER-oh

Nesib: NEE-zib

Nesroch: NES-rahk

Netaim: neh-TAY-im

Nethaneal: neh-THAN-ee-uhl

Nethaneel: neh-THAN-ee-uhl

Nethanel: neh-THAN-uhl

Nethaniah: NETH-uh-**NYE**-uh

Nethinim: NETH-in-im

Netopha: neh-TOH-fuh

Netophah: neh-TOH-fuh

Netophathi: neh-TAHF-uh-thye

Netophathite: neh-TAHF-uh-thite

Netophati: neh-TAHF-uh-tye

Neviim: neh-veh-EEM

Nevi'im: neh-veh-EEM

Neziah: neh-ZYE-uh

Nezib: NEE-zib

Nibhaz: NIB-haz

Nibshan: NIB-shan

Nicanor - nye-KAY-nuhr

Nicodemus: NIK-uh-**DEE**-muhs

Nicolaitan: NIK-uh-**LAY**-uh-tuhn

Nicolaitane: NIK-uh-**LAY**-uh-tayn

Nicolas: NIK-uh-luhs

Nicolaus: NIK-uh-**LAY**-uhs

Nicopolis: neh-KOP-uh-lis

Nidia: NID-ee-uh

Niger: NYE-guhr

Nile: nyel

Nimrah: NIM-ruh

Nimrim: NIM-rim

Nimrod: NIM-rahd

Nimshi: NIM-shye

Nineveh: NIN-eh-vuh

Ninevite: NIN-uh-vite

Ninive: NIN-eh-veh

Niphis: NIF-is

Nisan: NYE-san

Nisroch: NIS-rahk

Nisrok: NIS-rahk

Nissi: NIS-ee

nitre: NYE-tuhr

No: noh

Noa: NOH-uh

Noadiah: NOH-uh-**DYE**-uh

Noah: NOH-uh

No-amon: noh-AM-uhn

Nob: nahb

Nobah: NOH-buh

Nobai: NOH-bye

Nobe: NOH-buh

Nod: nahd

Nodab: NOH-dab

Nodan: NOH-dan

Noe: NOH-ee or NOH-uh

Noeba: noh-EE-buh

Noema: NOH-uh-muh

Noeman: NOH-uh-man

Noemi: NOH-uh-mye

Noga: NOH-guh

Nogah: NOH-guh

Noge: NOH-guh

Nohaa: noh-HAY-uh

Nohah: NOH-hah

Nohesta: noh-HES-tuh

Nohestan: noh-HES-tan

Non: nahn

Noph: nahf

Nophah: NOH-fuh

Nophe: NOH-fuh

Nopheth: NOH-feth

Noran: NOH-ruhn

Nubian: NOO-bee-uhn

Numbers: NUHM-buhrz

Numenius: noo-MEE-nee-uhs

Nun: nuhn

nun: nuhn

Nympha: NIM-fuh

Nymphas: NIM-fuhs

O

Obadia: OH-buh-**DYE**-uh

Obadiah: OH-buh **DYE**-uh

Obal: OH-buhl

Obdia: ohb-DYE-uh

Obdias: ohb-DYE-uhs

Obed: OH-behd

Obed-edom: OH-behd-**EE**-duhm

Obededom: OH-behd-**EE**-duhm

Obeth: OH-behth

Obil: OH-bil

obol: OH-buhl

Oboth: OH-bahth

Ochiel: oh-KYE-uhl

Ochozias: OH-kuh-**ZYE**-uhs

Ochran: AHK-ruhn

Ocidelus: oh-seh-DEE-luhs

Ocina: oh-SYE-nuh

Ocran: AHK-ruhn

Odaia: oh-DYE-uh

Odares: oh-DAY-reez

Oded: OH-dehd

Odoia: OH-duh-**EYE**-uh

Odollam: oh-DAHL-uhm

Odomera: AHD-uh-**MAIR**-uh

Odonarkes: AHD-uh-**NAHR**-keez

Oduia: OH-duh-**EYE**-uh

Odullam: oh-DAHL-uhm

Og: ahg

Ohad: OH-had

Oham: OH-ham

Ohel: OH-hel

Ohol: OH-hohl

Oholah: oh-HOH-luh

Oholai: oh-HOH-lye

Oholi: oh-HOH-lye

Oholiab: oh-HOH-lee-ab

Oholibah: oh-HOH-leh-buh

Oholibamah: oh-HOH-li-**BAH**-muh

Olamus: OH-luh-muhs

Olive: AHL-iv

Olivet: AHL-i-veht

Olla: AHL-uh

Olon: OH-luhn

Olympas: oh-LIM-puhs

Olympian: oh-LIM-pee-uhn

Olympius: oh-LIM-pee-uhs

Omaerus: oh-MEE-ruhs

Omar: OH-mahr

omega: oh-MAY-guh

omer: OH-muhr

omerful: OH-muhr-fuhl

Omrai: AHM-rye

Omri: AHM-rye

On: ahn

Onam: OH-nuhm

Onan: OH-nuhn

One: OH-nuh

Onesimus: oh-NES-uh-muhs

Onesiphorus: ON-uh-**SIF**-uh-ruhs

Oni: OH-nye

Onias: oh-NYE-uhs

Ono: OH-noh

Onus: OH-nuhs

onycha: AHN-i-kuh

Ooliba: oh-HOH-leh-buh

Oolibama: oh-HOH-li-**BAH**-muh

Oolla: oh-HOH-luh

Ophaz: OH-faz

Ophel: OH-fel

Opher: OH-fuhr

Ophera: OH-fuhr-uh

Ophi: OH-fye

Ophir: OH-fuhr

Ophlal: AHF-lal

Ophni: AHF-nye

Ophra: AHF-ruh

Ophrah: AHF-ruh

Oracle: OR-uh-kuhl

Oreb: OR-eb

Oregim: OH-ruh-gim

Oren: OR-en

Orion: oh-RYE-uhn

Ornan: OR-nuhn

Oronaim: OR-oh-**NAY**-im

Orori: oh-ROH-rye

Orpah: OR-puh

Orthosia: or-THOH-see-uh

Orthosias: or-THOH-see-uhs

Osaias: oh-SAY-uhs

Osea: oh-SEE-uh

Oseas: oh-SEE-uhs

Osee: OH-see

Oshea: oh-SHEE-uh

Osnapper: ahs-NAP-uhr

Othei: OH-thye

Othni: AHTH-nye

Othniel: AHTH-nee-uhl

Otholia: AHTH-uh-**LYE**-uh

Othoniah: AHTH-uh-**NYE**-uh

Othonias: AHTH-uh-**NYE**-uhs

Othoniel: oh-THAH-nee-uhl

Orthosias: or-THOH-see-us

Ox: ohks

Oza: AHZ-uh

Ozam: OH-zuhm

Ozan: OZ-zuhn

Ozaziu: AHZ-uh-**ZYE**-oo

Ozem: OH-zuhm

Ozensara: AHZ-uhn-**SAHR**-uh

Ozi: AHZ-eye

Ozia: oh-ZYE-uh

Ozial: OH-zee-uhl

Ozias: oh-ZYE-uhs

Oziel: OH-zee-uhl

Ozielite: oh-ZEE-uh-lite

Ozni: AHZ-nye

Oznite: AHZ-nite

Ozora: oh-ZOR-uh

P

Paaneah: PAY-uh-**NEE**-uh

Paarai: PAY-uh-rye

Paari: PAY-uh-rye

Pacatania: PAK-uh-**TAN**-ee-uh

Pachon: PAY-kuhn

Padan: PAY-duhn

Padan Aram: PAY-duhn-**AIR**-uhm

Padan-aram: PAY-duhn-**AIR**-uhm

Paddan: PAD-uhn

Paddan Aram: PAD-uhn-**AIR**-uhm

Paddan-aram: PAD-uhn-**AIR**-uhm

Padon: PAY-duhn

Pagiel: PAY-gee-uhl

Pahath-moab: PAY-hath-**MOH**-ab

Pahathmoab: PAY-hath-**MOH**-ab

Pai: pye

Palal: PAY-lal

Palestina: PAL-uh-**STYE**-nuh

Palestine: PAL-uh-styne

Palet: PAY-lit

Pallu: PAL-yoo

Palluite: PAL-yoo-ite

Palmira: pal-MEER-uh

Palti: PAL-tye

Paltiel: PAL-tee-uhl

Paltite: PAL-tite

Pamphylia: pam-FIL-ee-yuh

Pannag: PAN-ag

Paphos: PAY-fahs

parable: PAIR-uh-buhl

Paraclete: PAIR-uh-kleet

Paradise: PAIR-uh-dyse

Parah: PAY-ruh

Paralipomenon: PAIR-uh-leh-**PAHM**-uh-nahn

Paran: PAY-ruhn

Parath: PAY-ruhth

Parbar: PAHR-bahr

Parmashta: pahr-MASH-tuh

Parmenas: PAHR-muh-nuhs

Parnach: PAHR-nak

Parosh: PAY-rahsh

Parshandatha: pahr-SHAN-duh-thuh

parsin: PAHR-sin

Parthia: PAHR-thee-uh

Parthian: PAHR-thee-uhn

Paruah: puh-ROO-uh

Parvaim: pahr-VAY-im

Parzite: PAHR-zite

Pas: pas

Pasach: PAY-sak

pasch: pask

Paschal: PAS-kuhl

Pas Dammim: pas-DAM-im

Pas-dammim: pas-DAM-im

Pasdammim: pas-DAM-im

Paseah: puh-SEE-uh

Pashhur: PASH-huhr

Pashur: PASH-uhr

Passover: PAS-oh-vuhr

Patara: PAT-uh-ruh

Patheus: puh-THEE-uhs

Pathros: PATH-rahs

Pathrus: PATH-ruhs

Pathrusim: path-ROO-sim

Pathrusite: path-ROO-site

Patmos: PAT-muhs

Patrobas: PAT-ruh-buhs

Patroclus: puh-TROH-kluhs

Pau: pou

Paul: pawl

Paulus: PAW-luhs

Pazzez: PAZ-iz

pe: pay

Pedahel: PED-uh-hel

Pedahzur: peh-DAH-zuhr

Pedaiah: peh-DAY-uh

peh: pay

Pekah: PEE-kuh

Pekahiah: PEK-uh-**HYE**-uh

Pekod: PEE-kahd

Pelaiah: peh-LAY-uh

Pelaliah: PEL-uh-**LYE**-uh

Pelatiah: PEL-uh-**TYE**-uh

Peleg: PEE-leg

Pelet: PEE-let

Peleth: PEE-leth

Pelethite: PEL-uh-thite

Pelias: PEL-ee-uhs

Pelon: PEE-luhn

Pelonite: PEE-luh-nite

Pelusium: peh-LOO-see-uhm

Peniel: PEN-ee-uhl

Peninnah: peh-NIN-uh

Pentapolis: pen-TAP-uh-lis

Pentecost: PEN-teh-kahst

Penuel: peh-NEW-uhl

Peor: PEE-or

Perath: PEE-rath

Perazim: peh-RAY-zim

perdition: per-DI-shuhn

Peres: PEE-res

Peresh: PEE-resh

Perez: PEE-rez

Perezite: PER-uh-zite

Perez-uzza: PEE-riz-**UH**-zuh

Perezuzza: PEE-riz-**UH**-zuh

Perez Uzzah: PEE-riz-**UH**-zuh

Perez-uzzah: PEE-riz-**UH**-zuh

Perezuzzah: PEE-riz-**UH**-zuh

Perga: PUHR-guh

Pergamos: PUHR-guh-muhs

Pergamum: PUHR-guh-muhm

Perida: peh-RYE-duh

Perizzite: PUHR-eh-zite

Persepolis: puhr-SEP-uh-lis

Perses: PUHR-seez

Perseus: PUHR-see-uhs

Persia: PUHR-zhuh

Persian: PUHR-zhuhn

Persis: PUHR-sis

Peruda: peh-ROO-duh

Peter: PEE-tuhr

Pethahiah: PETH-uh-**HYE**-uh

Pethor: PEE-thor

Pethuel: peh-THYOO-uhl

Petra: PET-ruh

Peullethai: peh-OOL-uh-thye

Peulthai: peh-OOL-thye

Phaath Moab: FAY-ath-**MOH**-ab

Phacareth: FAK-uh-reth

Phacee: FAY-see

Phaceia: fuh-SEE-uh

Phadaia: fuh-DYE-uh

Phadassur: fuh-DAH-zuhr

Phadoura: fuh-DOOR-uh

Phaisur: FAY-zuhr

Phalaris: FAL-uh-ruhs

Phaldaius: fal-DAY-uhs

Phaleas: fuh-LEE-uhs

Phalec: FAY-lek

Phaleg: FAY-leg

Phalet: FAY-let

Phaleth: FAY-leth

Phallet: FAY-let

Phallu: FAL-oo

Phalonite: FAL-uh-nite

Phalti: FAL-tye

Phaltias: fal-TYE-uhs

Phaltiel: FAL-tee-uhl

Phanuel: fuh-NEW-uhl

Phara: FAIR-uh

Pharai: FAIR-eye

Pharakim: FAIR-uh-kim

Pharam: FAIR-uhm

Pharan: FAIR-uhn

Pharaoh: FAIR-oh

Pharaoh-hophra: FAIR-oh-**HOF**-ruh

Pharaoh-necho: FAIR-oh-**NEE**-koh

Pharaoh-nechoh: FAIR-oh-**NEE**-koh

Pharaoh Neco: FAIR-oh-**NEE**-koh

Pharaoh-neco: FAIR-oh-**NEE**-koh

Pharathon: FAIR-uh-thon

Pharathoni: FAIR-uh-**THOH**-nye

Pharathonite: FAIR-uh-**THOH**-nite

Phares: FAIR-is

Pharez: FAIR-iz

Pharira: fuh-RYE-ruh

Pharisaic: FAIR-uh-**SAY**-ik

Pharisee: FAIR-uh-see

Pharnach: FAIR-nak

Pharosh: FAY-rahsh

Pharpar: FAHR-pahr

Pharphar: FAHR-pahr

Pharue: fuh-ROO-uh

Pharurim: fuh-ROO-rim

Pharzite: FAHR-zite

Phaseah: fuh-SEE-uh

Phaselis: fuh-SEE-lis

Phaseron: FAS-uh-rahn

Phasiron: FAS-uh-rahn

Phasga: FAS-guh

Phaspha: FAS-fuh

Phassaron: FAS-uh-rahn

Phassur: FAS-uhr

Phatuel: fuh-TEW-uhl

Phatures: fuh-TEW-rez

Phau: FAY-oo

phe: fay

Phebe: FEE-bee

Phedael: FED-uh-el

Phegiel: fuh-GEE-el

Pheleia: fuh-LAY-uh

Phelet: FEE-let

Pheleth: FEE-leth

Phelethi: FEE-luh-thye

Pheltias: fel-TYE-uhs

Phenenna: fuh-NEN-nuh

Phenice: feh-NYE-see

Phenicia: feh-NYE-shee-uh

Pherez: FAIR-ez

Pherezite: FAIR-uh-zite

Pherizite: FAIR-uh-zite

Phesdomim: fez-DAHM-im

Phesse: fuh-SEE-uh

Phetros: FET-rahs

Phetrusim: feh-TROO-sim

Phibeseth: FYE-buh-seth

Phichol: FYE-kahl

Phicol: FYE-kahl

Phihahiroth: FYE-hah-**HYE**-ruhth

Philadelphia: FIL-uh-**DEL**-fee-uh

Philarches: fil-AHR-keez

Philemon: feh-LEE-muhn

Philetus: feh-LEE-tuhs

Philip: FIL-ip

Philippi: fi-LIP-eye or FIL-eh-pye

Philippians: fi-LIP-ee-uhnz

Philistia: fi-LIS-tee-uh

Philistim: fi-LIS-tim

Philistine: fi-LIS-teen

Philologus: fil-AHL-uh-guhs

Philometor: FIL-uh-**MEE**-tor

Philopator: FIL-uh-**PAY**-tor

Phineas: FIN-ee-uhs

Phinees: FIN-ee-uhs

Phinehas: FIN-ee-huhs

Phinoi: FIN-oi

Phinon: FYE-nuhn

Phison: FYE-sahn

Phithon: FYE-thuhn

Phlegon: FLEG-uhn

Phoebe: FEE-bee

Phoenice: fi-NYE-see

Phoenicia: fi-NISH-uh

Phoenician: fi-NISH-uhn

Phoenix: FEE-niks

Phogor: FOH-gor

Phoros: FOR-ahs

Phosech: FOH-sek

Phrygia: FRIJ-ee-uh

Phrygian: FRIJ-ee-uhn

Phua: FEW-uh

Phud: fuhd

Phul: fuhl

Phunon: FEW-nuhn

Phurah: FEW-ruh

Phurim: FEW-rim

Phut: fuht

Phuvah: FEW-vuh

Phygellus: fi-JEL-uhs

Phygelus: FYE-juh-luhs

phylarch: FYE-lahrk

Pi: pye

Pi Beseth: pye-BEE-sith

Pi-beseth: pye-BEE-sith

Pibeseth: pye-BEE-sith

Pi Hahiroth: PYE-huh-**HYE**-rahth

Pi-hahiroth: PYE-huh-**HYE**-rahth

Pihahiroth: PYE-huh-**HYE**-rahth

Pilate: PYE-luht

Pildash: PIL-dash

Pileha: PIL-uh-hah

Pileser: pi-LEE-suhr

Pilha: PIL-hah

Pilneser: pil-NEE-suhr

Piltai: PIL-tye

pim: pim

Pinon: PYE-nahn

Pira: PYE-ruh

Piram: PYE-ruhm

Pirathon: PEER-uh-thahn

Pirathonite: PEER-uh-thuh-nite

Pisgah: PIZ-guh

Pishon: PYE-shahn

Pisidia: pi-SID-ee-uh
Pisidian: pi-SID-ee-uhn
Pisidian Antioch: pi-SID-ee-uhn-**AN**-tee-ahk
Pison: PYE-suhn
Pispa: PIS-puh
Pispah: PIS-puh
Pithom: PYE-thahm
Pithon: PYE-thahn
Pleiades: PLEE-uh-deez
Pochereth: PAHK-uh-reth
Pochereth-hazzebaim: PAHK-uh-reth-haz-uh-**BAY**-im
Pocherethhazzebaim: PAHK-uh-reth-haz-uh-**BAY**-im
Pokereth-hazzebaim: PAHK-uh-reth-haz-uh-**BAY**-im
Pollux: PAHL-uhks
Pontius: PAHN-shuhs
Pontus: PAHN-tuhs
Poratha: por-AY-thuh
Porathai: por-AY-thye
Porcius: POR-shuhs
porphyrion: por-FYE-ree-ahn
Posidonius: PAHS-uh-**DOH**-nee-uhs
Poti: POH-tye
Potiphar: POT-uh-fuhr
Potiphera: puh-TI-fuh-ruh
Poti-pherah: puh-TI-fuh-ruh
Praetorian: pri-TOR-ee-uhn
Praetorium: pri-TOR-ee-uhn
Preacher: PREE-chuhr
prefect: PREE-fekt
presbyter: PRES-beh-tuhr
presbytery: **PRES**-beh-TER-ee
Pretorium: pri-TOR-ee-uhm
Priapus: PRYE-uh-puhs
Prisca: PRIS-kuh
Priscilla: pri-SIL-uh

Prochorus: PRAHK-uh-ruhs

proconsul: proh-KAHN-suhl

proconsular: proh-KAHN-suh-luhr

Procorus: PRAHK-uh-ruhs

procurator: **PRAHK**-yuh-RAY-tuhr

Prophet: PRAHF-it

proselyte: PRAHS-uh-lite

Proverb: PRAHV-uhrb

Psalm: sahm

psaltery: SAWL-tuh-ree

Ptolemaic: TAHL-uh-**MAY**-ik

Ptolemais: TAHL-uh-**MAY**-uhs

Ptolemeans: TAHL-uh-**MAY**-uhns

Ptolemee: TAHL-uh-mee

Ptolemy: TAHL-uh-mee

Pua: PEW-uh

Puah: PEW-uh

publican: PUHB-li-kuhn

Publius: PUHB-lee-uhs

Pudens: PEW-denz

Puhite: PEW-hite

Puite: PEW-ite

Pul: puhl

Punite: PEW-nite

Punon: PEW-nahn

Pur: pewr

Purah: PEW-ruh

Purim: PEW-rim

Put: poot

Puteoli: pew-TEE-oh-lee

Puthite: PEW-thite

Putiel: PEW-tee-uhl

Puvah: PEW-vuh

Puvahite: PEW-vuh-hite

Puvvah: POO-vuh

pygarg: PIG-ahrg

Pygmean: pig-MEE-uhn

Pyrrhus: PEER-uhs

Q

Qoheleth: koh-HEL-ith

qoph: kohf

quadrans: KWAD-ruhns

Quartus: KWOR-tuhs

quaternion: kwah-TUHR-nee-uhn

Quintus: KWIN-tuhs

Quirinius: kwi-RIN-ee-uhs

R

Raama: RAY-uh-mah

Raamah: RAY-uh-mah

Raamiah: RAY-uh-**MYE**-uh

Raamses: ray-AM-seez

Rab: rab

Rabba: RAB-uh

Rabbah: RAB-uh

Rabbath: RAB-uhth

rabbi: RAB-eye

Rabbim: RAB-im

Rabbith: RAB-ith

rabboni: rah-BOH-nye

Rabboth: RAB-ith

rabbouni: rah-BOO-nye

Rabmag: RAB-mag

Rab-mag: RAB-mag

Rabsaces: RAB-shuh-seez

Rabsares: RAB-suh-res

Rabsaris: RAB-suh-ris

Rab-saris: RAB-suh-ris

Rab-shakeh: RAB-shuh-kuh

Rabshakeh: RAB-shuh-kuh

raca: RAH-kah

Racal: RAY-kuhl

Rachab: RAY-kab

Rachal: RAY-kuhl

Rachel: RAY-chuhl

Raddai: RAD-eye

Ragab: RAY-hab

Ragae: RAY-gee

Ragau: RAY-gaw

Rages: RAH-guhs

Raguel: ruh-GEW-uhl

Rahab-hem-shebeth: RAY-hab-hem-**SHEE**-beth

Raham: RAY-huhm

Rahel: RAY-hel

Rahm: rahm

Rahuel: ruh-HEW-uhl

Raia: ray-EYE-uh

Rakem: RAY-kem

Rakkath: RAK-uhth

Rakkon: RAK-ahn

Ram: ram

Rama: RAY-muh

Ramah: RAY-muh

Ramath: RAY-muhth

Ramatha: RAY-muh-thuh

Ramathaim: RAM-uh-**THAY**-im

Ramathaimsophim: RAM-uh-THAY-im-**SOH**-fim

Ramathaim Zophim: RAM-uh-THAY-im-**ZOH**-fim

Ramathaim-zophim: RAM-uh-THAY-im-**ZOH**-fim

Ramathaimzophim: RAM-uh-THAY-im-**ZOH**-fim

Ramathem: RAM-uh-thim

Ramathite: RAY-muh-thite

Ramathlechi: RAY-muhth-**LEE**-kye

Ramath Lehi: RAY-muhth-**LEE**-hye

Ramath-lehi: RAY-muhth-**LEE**-hye

Ramathlehi: RAY-muhth-**LEE**-hye

Ramath Mizpah: RAY-muhth-**MIZ**-puh

Ramath-mizpah: RAY-muhth-**MIZ**-puh

Ramath-mizpeh: RAY-muhth-**MIZ**-puh

Ramathmizpeh: RAY-muhth-**MIZ**-puh

Rameses: RAM-uh-seez

Ramesses: RAM-uh-seez

Rameth: RAY-meth

Ramiah: ruh-MYE-uh

Ramoth: RAY-mahth

Ramoth Gilead: RAY-muhth-**GIL**-ee-uhd

Ramoth-gilead: RAY-muhth-**GIL**-ee-uhd

Ramothgilead: RAY-muhth-**GIL**-ee-uhd

Ramoth-negeb: RAY-muhth-**NEG**-eb

Ramoth Negev: RAY-muhth-**NEG**-ev

Rapha: RAY-fuh

Raphael: RAF-ay-uhl

Raphah: RAY-fuh

Raphaia: ruh-FAY-uh

Raphaim: RAF-ay-im

Raphain: RAF-ay-in

Raphia: ruh-FYE-uh

Raphidim: RAF-uh-dim

Raphon: RAY-fahn

Raphu: RAY-few

Rasin: RAY-sin

Rasses: RAS-eez

Rassis: RAS-is

Rassisite: RAS-i-site

Rathamin: RATH-uh-min

Rathumus: ruh-THEW-muhs

Razias: ray-ZYE-uhs

Razis: RAY-zis

Razon: RAY-zahn

Reaia: ree-AY-uh

Reaiah: ree-AY-uh

Reba: REE-buh

Rebe: REE-buh

Rebecca: reh-BEK-uh

Rebekah: reh-BEK-uh

Rebla: REB-luh

Reblatha: REB-luh-thuh

Rebmag: REB-mag

Recab: REE-kab

Recabite: REK-uh-bite

Recah: REE-kuh

Reccath: RAK-uth

Recem: REE-kem

Recen: RAY-ken

Recha: REE-kuh

Rechah: REE-kuh

Rechab: REE-kab

Rechabite: REK-uh-bite

Reema: RAY-uh-muh

Regem: REE-gum

Regem-melech: REE-gum-**MEE**-lick

Regma: RAY-uh-muh

Rehob: REE-hob

Rehoboam: REH-hoh-**BOH**-uhm

Rehoboth: reh-HOH-bahth

Rehoboth Ir: reh-**HOH**-bahth-EER

Rei: REE-eye

Reia: ruh-EYE-uh

Rekabite: REK-uh-bite

Rekem: REE-kem

Remaliah: REM-uh-**LYE**-uh

Remeth: REE-mith

Remmon: REM-uhn

Remmono: REM-uhn

Remmomphares: REM-uhm-**PEE**-rez

Rephah: REE-fuh

Rephaiah: reh-FAY-uh

Rephaim: ref-AY-im

Rephaite: reh-FAY-ite

Rephidim: REF-uh-dim

res: raysh

Resen: REES-en

Reseph: REE-sef

resh: raysh

Resheph: REE-shef

Resia: RIZ-ee-uh

Respha: RIZ-puh

Ressa: RES-uh

Rethma: RETH-muh

Reu: REE-oo

Reuben: ROO-ben

Reuel: ROO-uhl

Reumah: ROO-muh

Revelation: REV-uh-**LAY**-shuhn

Rezeph: REE-zif

Rezia: reh-ZYE-uh

Rezin: REE-zin

Rezon: REE-zuhn

Rhegium: REE-jee-uhm

Rhesa: REE-suh

Rhoda: ROH-duh

Rhodanite: ROH-duh-nite

Rhodes: rohdz

Rhodocus: RAHD-uh-kuhs

Ribai: RYE-bye

Riblah: RIB-luh

Rimmon: RIM-uhn

Rimmono: ri-MOH-nuh

Rimmon-parez: RIM-uhn-**PAY**-riz

Rimmon Perez: RIM-uhn-**PEE**-riz

Rimmon-perez: RIM-uhn-**PEE**-riz

Rimmonperez: RIM-uhn-**PEE**-riz

Rinna: RIN-nuh

Rinnah: RIN-nuh

Riphath: RYE-fath

Rishathaim: RISH-uh-**THAY**-im

Rissah: RIS-uh

Rithmah: RITH-muh

Rizia: ri-ZYE-uh

Rizpah: RIZ-puh

Roaga: ROH-guh

Roboam: roh-BOH-uhm

Rodanim: ROH-duh-nim

Rogel: ROH-guhl

Rogelim: ROH-guh-lim

Rogom: ROH-gahm

Rogommelech: ROH-gahm-**MEE**-lik

Rohgah: ROH-guh

Rohob: ROH-hahb

Rohoboth: roh-HOH-bahth

Rohol: ROH-hahl

Roi: roi

Roimus: ROH-i-muhs

Romamti-ezer: roh-MAM-ti-**EE**-zuhr

Romamtiezer: roh-MAM-ti-**EE**-zuhr

Roman: ROH-muhn

Rome: rohm

Romelia: ROHM-uh-**LYE**-uh

Rompha: ROHM-fuh

Rosh: rahsh

Ruben: ROO-bin

rue: roo

Rufus: ROO-fuhs

Ruhama: roo-HAY-muh

Ruhamah: roo-HAY-muh

Ruma: ROO-muh

Rumah: ROO-muh

Ruth: rooth

S

Saananim: SAY-uh-**NAN**-im

Saaph: SAY-af

Saaphan: SAY-uh-fuhn

Saarim: SAY-uh-rim

Saba: SAY-buh

Sabachai: SAB-uh-kye

sabachthani: suh-BAK-thuh-nye

Sabama: suh-BAY-muh

Saban: SAY-ban

Sabaoth: SAB-ay-ahth

Sabarim: SAB-uh-rim

Sabat: SAB-uht

Sabateas: SAB-uh-**TEE**-uhs

Sabatha: SAB-uh-thuh

Sabathaca: SAB-uh-**THAY**-kuh

Sabatus: SAB-uh-tuhs

Sabbaias: suh-BAY-uhs

Sabban: SAB-an

Sabbath: SAB-uhth

Sabbatheus: SAB-uh-**THEE**-uhs

sabbatical: suh-BAT-i-kuhl

Sabbeus: suh-BEE-uhs

Sabean: suh-BEE-uhn

Sabee: suh-BEE-uh

Saber: SAY-buhr

Sabi: SAY-bye

Sabta: SAB-tuh

Sabtah: SAB-tuh

Sabteca: SAB-tuh-kuh or sab-TEE-kuh

Sabtecah: SAB-tuh-kuh or sab-TEE-kuh

Sabtecha: SAB-tuh-kuh or sab-TEE-kuh

Sabtechah: SAB-tuh-kuh or sab-TEE-kuh

Sacar: SAY-kahr

Sachacha: suh-KAY-kuh

Sachar: SAY-kahr

Sachia: suh-KYE-uh

Sadamias: SAD-uh-**MYE**-uhs

Sadas: SAY-duhs

Saddeus: SAD-ee-uhs

Sadduc: SAD-uhk

Sadducee: SAD-joo-see

Sadduk: SAD-uhk

sade: SAH-day

sadhe: SAH-day

Sadoc: SAY-dahk

Sage: SAY-guh

Sahar: SAY-hahr

Saharim: SAY-huh-rim

Sais: syes

Sakia: suh-KYE-uh

Sakkuth: SAK-uhth

Sala: SAY-luh

Salaboni: **SAY**-luh-BOH-nye

Salabonite: **SAY**-luh-BOH-nite

Salah: SAY-luh

Salai: SAY-lye

Salamiel: suh-LAY-mee-uhl

Salamis: SAL-uh-mis

Salasadai: SAL-uh-**SAD**-eye

Salathi: SAL-uh-thye

Salathiel: suh-LAY-thee-uhl

Salcah: SAL-kuh

Salchah: SAL-kuh

Sale: SAL-uh

Salebim: SAL-uh-bim

Salecah: SAL-uh-kuh

Salecha: SAL-uh-kuh

Saled: SAY-led

Salekah: SAL-uh-kuh

Salem: SAY-luhm

Saleph: SAY-lef

Salim: SAY-lim

Salisa: SAL-is-uh

Sallai: SAL-eye

Sallu: SAL-oo

Sallumus: SAL-uh-muhs

Salma: SAL-muh

Salmai: SAL-mye

Salman: SAL-man

Salmana: sal-MAN-uh

Salmanasar: SAL-man-**AY**-sahr

Salmon: SAL-muhn

Salmona: sal-MOH-nuh

Salmone: sal-MOH-nee

Salo: SAL-oo

Salom: SAY-luhm

Salome: suh-LOH-mee

Salomi: suh-LOH-mye

Salomith: suh-LOH-mith

Salphaad: sal-FAY-ad

Saltus: SAHL-tuhs

Salu: SAY-loo

Salum: SAY-luhm

Salusa: suh-LOO-suh

Sama: SAM-muh

Samaa: SAM-ay-uh

Samaan: SAM-ay-uhn

Samad: SAM-ad

Samae: SAM-ee-uh

Samael: SAM-ay-uhl

Samaia: suh-MAY-uh

Samaias: suh-MAY-uhs

Samaraim: SAM-uh-**RAY**-im

Samareth: SAM-uh-reth

Samaria: suh-MAIR-ee-uh

Samarian: suh-MAIR-ee-uhn

Samaritan: suh-MAIR-uh-tuhn

Samarite: SAM-uh-rite

Samatus: suh-MAY-tuhs

samech: SAH-mek

Sameius: suh-MEE-uhs

samekh: SAH-mek

Samgar: SAM-gahr

Samgar-nebo: SAM-gahr **NEE**-boh

Samgarnebo: SAM-gahr **NEE**-boh

Samgar-nebu: SAM-gahr **NEE**-boo

Sami: SAY-mye

Samir: SAY-muhr

Samis: SAY-mis

Samlah: SAM-luh

Samma: SAM-uh

Sammaa: suh-MAY-uh

Sammai: suh-MAY-eye

Sammoth: SAM-ahth

Sammua: sam-YOO-uh

Sammus: SAM-uhs

Samoa: sam-OH-uh

Samos: SAY-mahs

Samothrace: SAM-uh-thrays

Samothracia: SAM-uh-**THRAY**-shuh

Sampsames: SAMP-suh-meez

Samsari: SAM-suh-rye

Samson: SAM-suhn

Samua: sam-YOO-uh

Samuel: SAM-yoo-uhl

Samus: SAY-muhs

Sanabassar: SAN-uh-**BAS**-uhr

Sanabassarus: SAN-uh-**BAS**-uh-ruhs

Sanan: SAY-nuhn

Sanasib: SAN-uh-sib

Sanballat: san-BAL-at

Sanhedrin: san-HEE-druhn

Sanir: SAY-neer

Sansannah: san-SAN-uh

Saph: saf

Saphai: SAF-ay-eye

Sapham: SAY-fuhm

Saphan: SAY-fan

Saphat: SAY-fat

Saphathia: SAF-uh-**THYE**-uh

Saphatia: SAF-uh-**TYE**-uh

Saphatias: SAF-uh-**TYE**-uhs

Sapheth: SAY-fith

Saphir: SAY-fuhr

Sapphira: suh-FYE-ruh

Sara: SAIR-uh

Saraa: suh-RAY-uh

Sarabias: SAIR-uh-**BYE**-uhs

Sarah: SAIR-uh

Sarai: SAIR-eye

Saraia: suh-RYE-uh

Saraias: suh-RAY-uhs

Saraim: suh-RAY-im

Saraite: suh-RAY-ite

Saramel: SAIR-uh-mel

Saraph: SAIR-uhf

Sarar: SAY-ruhr

Sarasadai: SAIR-uh-**SAD**-eye

Sarasar: SAIR-uh-sahr

Sarathasar: sair-uh-**THAY**-suhr

Sarathi: SAIR-ruh-thye

Sarchedonus: SAHR-kuh-**DOH**-nuhs

Sardeus: sahr-DEE-uhs

Sardis: SAHR-dis

Sardite: SAHR-dite

sardius: SAHR-dee-uhs

sardonyx: sahr-DAHN-iks

Sarea: SAIR-ee-uh

Sareas: SAIR-ee-uhs

Sared: SAIR-uhd

Sareda: SAIR-uh-duh

Sarephta: suh-REF-tuh

Sarepta: suh-REP-tuh

Sares: SAIR-es

Sargon: SAHR-gahn

Saria: suh-RYE-uh

Sarid: SAIR-id

Sarion: suh-RYE-uhn

Saris: SAIR-is

Sarohen: suh-ROH-uhn

Saron: SAIR-uhn

Sarothie: suh-ROH-thee

Sarsachim: SAHR-suh-kim

Sar-sechim: SAHR-suh-kim

Sarsechim: SAHR-suh-kim

Sartham: SAHR-thuhm

Sarthan: SAHR-thuhn

Sarthana: sahr-THAN-uh

Sarua: suh-ROO-uh

Saruch: SAIR-uhk

Sarvia: SAHR-vee-uh

Satan: SAY-tuhn

Sathra-buzanes: SATH-ruh-**BEW**-zuh-neez

Sathrabuzanes: SATH-ruh-**BEW**-zuh-neez

satrap: SAY-trap

satrapy: SAY-truh-pee

Saul: sawl

Saura: SAHR-uh

Savaran: SAV-uh-ruhn

Save: SAY-vuh

Savias: suh-VYE-uhs

Scenopegia: SEEN-oh-**PEE**-jee-uh

Sceva: SEE-vuh

Schedia: shuh-DYE-uh

schin: shin

Scripture: SKRIP-chuhr

Scibboleth: SHIB-oh-leth

Sciniph: SIN-if

Scythian: SITH-ee-uhn

Scythopolis: sith-AHP-uh-lis

Scythopolitan: sith-uh-PAHL-eh-tuhn

seah: SEE-uh

Seba: SEE-buh

Sebam: SEE-bam

Sebat: SEE-bat

Sebenias: SEB-uh-nye-uhs

Sebeon: SEB-ee-uhn

Sebia: suh-BYE-uh

Seboim: seh-BOI-im

Secacah: seh-KAY-kuh

Sechem: SEK-im

Sechenias: SEK-uh-**NYE**-uhs

Sechia: suh-KYE-uh

Sechrona: sek-ROH-nuh

Sechu: SEE-kew

Secu: SEE-kew

Secundus: seh-KOON-duhs

Sedada: see-DAD-uh

Sedecias: SED-uh-**KYE**-uhs

Sedei: seh-DEE-eye

Sedeur: seh-DEE-uhr

Sedi: SEE-dye

Seen: SEE-uhn

Segor: SEE-gahr

Segub: SEE-guhb

Sehesima: SAY-huh-**SYE**-muh

Sehon: SAY-hahn

Seir: SEE-uhr

Seira: SEE-uh-ruh

Seirah: SEE-uh-ruh

Seirath: SEE-uh-rath

Sela: SEE-luh

Selah: SEE-luh

selah: SEE-luh

Sela Hammahlekoth: SEE-luh-huh-**MAH**-luh-kahth

Sela-hammahlekoth: SEE-luh-huh-**MAH**-luh-kahth

Selcha: SEL-kuh

Selebin: SEE-luh-bin

Selec: SEE-lik

Seled: SEE-lid

Selemia: SEL-uh-**MYE**-uh

Selemias: SEL-uh-**MYE**-uhs

Selethai: SEL-uh-**THAY**-eye

Seleucia: seh-LOO-shuh

Seleucus: seh-LOO-kuhs

Selim: SEL-im

Sella: SEL-uh

Sellem: SEL-em

Selles: SEL-es

Sellum: SEL-uhm

Selmon: SEL-muhn

Sem: sem

Semaath: seh-MAY-ath

Semachiah: SEM-uh-**KYE**-uh

Semakiah: SEM-uh-**KYE**-uh

Semei: SEM-ee-eye

Semeia: SEM-ee-**EYE**-uh

Semeias: SEM-ee-**EYE**-uhs

Semein: SEM-ee-uhn

Semeite: SEM-ee-ite

Semellius: seh-MEL-ee-uhs

Semer: SEE-muhr

Semeron: SEM-uh-rahn

Semegarnabu: SEM-gahr-**NAY**-boo

Semida: sem-EYE-duh

Semiramoth: seh-MEER-uh-mahth

Semis: SEE-mis

Semla: SEM-luh

Semma: SEM-muh

Semran: SEM-ran

Semri: SEM-rye

Sen: sen

Senaah: suh-NAY-uh

Senate: SEN-it

Seneh: SEE-nuh

Senir: SEE-nuhr

Senna: SEN-uh

Sennaar: seh-NAY-ahr

Sennacherib: suh-NAK-uh-rib

Senneser: sen-NEE-zuhr

Sennim: SEN-im

Sensenna: sen-SEN-uh

Senuah: seh-NEW-uh

Seon: SEE-ahn

Seorim: see-OR-im

Sephaath: see-FAY-ath

Sepham: SEE-fam

Sephama: see-FAM-uh

Sephar: SEE-fuhr

Sepharad: SEF-uh-rad

Sephar-vaim: SEF-uhr-**VAY**-im

Sepharvaim: SEF-uhr-**VAY**-im

Sepharvite: SEF-uhr-vite

Sephatiah: SEF-uh-**TYE**-uh

Sephei: SEF-eye

Sephela: seh-FEE-luh

Sepher: SEE-fuhr

Sephi: SEE-fye

Sephon: SEE-fahn

Sephor: SEE-for

Sephtan: SEF-tan

Sephuphan: seh-FEW-fan

Ser: zuhr

Serah: SEER-uh

Seraiah: seh-RAY-uh

Seraias: seh-RAY-uhs

seraph: SAIR-uhf

seraphim: SAIR-uh-fim

Sered: SEER-id

Seredite: SEER-uh-dite

Sereth: SEE-reth

Sergius: SUHR-jee-uhs

Sergius Paulus: SUHR-jee-uhs-**PAW**-luhs

Seron: SEER-on

Seror: SEER-or

Serug: SEER-uhg

Sesac: SEE-sak

Sesai: SEE-sye

Sesan: SEE-san

Sesis: SEE-sis

Sesthel: SES-thuhl

Seth: seth

Sethur: SEE-thuhr

Setim: SET-im

Settim: SET-im

Seveneh: suh-VEN-uh

Shaalabbin: SHAY-uh-**LAB**-uhn

Shaalbim: shay-AL-bim

Shaalbon: shay-AL-bahn

Shaalbonite: shay-AL-buh-nite

Shaalim: SHAY-uh-lim

Shaaph: SHAY-af

Shaaraim: SHAY-uh-**RAY**-im

Shaashgaz: shay-ASH-gaz

Shabbethai: SAHB-uh-thye

Shachia: shuh-KYE-uh

Shaddai: SHAD-eye

Shadday: SHAD-eye

Shadrach: SHAD-rak

Shage: SHAY-geh

Shagee: SHAY-gee

Shageh: SHAY-geh

Shahar: SHAY-hahr

Shaharaim: SHAY-huh-**RAY**-im

Shahazimah: SHAY-huh-**ZYE**-muh

Shahazumah: SHAY-huh-**ZOO**-muh

Shakeh: SHAY-kuh

Shalal: SHAY-luhl

Shalem: SHAY-luhm

Shalim: SHAY-lim

Shalisha: shuh-LYE-shuh

Shalishah: shuh-LYE-shuh

Shallecheth: SHAL-uh-keth

Shalleketh: SHAL-uh-keth

Shallum: SHAL-uhm

Shallun: SHAL-uhn

Shalmai: SHAL-mye

Shalman: SHAL-muhn

Shalmaneser: SHAL-muh-**NEE**-zuhr

Shalom: shah-LOHM

Shama: SHAY-muh

Shamariah: SHAM-uh-**RYE**-uh

Shamed: SHAY-med

Shamer: SHAY-muhr

Shamgar: SHAM-gahr

Shamhuth: SHAM-huhth

Shamir: SHAY-muhr

Shamlai: SHAM-lye

Shamma: SHAM-uh

Shammah: SHAM-uh

Shammai: SHAM-eye

Shammoth: SHAM-ahth

Shammua: SHAH-mew-uh

Shammuah: SHAH-mew-uh

Shamsherai: SHAM-shuh-rye

Shan: shan

Shapham: SHAY-fuhm

Shaphan: SHAY-fuhn

Shaphat: SHAY-fat

Shapher: SHAY-fuhr

Shaphir: SHAY-fuhr

Sharai: SHAIR-eye

Sharaim: shuh-RAY-im

Sharar: SHAIR-ahr

Sharezer: shuh-REE-zuhr

Sharon: SHAIR-uhn

Sharonite: SHAIR-uh-nite

Sharuhen: shuh-ROO-huhn

Shashai: SHAY-shye

Shashak: SHAY-shak

Shaul: shawl

Shaulite: SHAW-lite

Shaveh: SHAY-vuh

Shaveh Kiriathaim: SHAY-vuh-keer-uh-**THAY**-im

Shaveh-kiriathaim: SHAY-vuh-keer-uh-**THAY**-im

Shavehkiriathaim: SHAY-vuh-keer-uh-**THAY**-im

Shavsha: SHAY-shuh

Shawsha: SHAW-shuh

Sheal: SHEE-uhl

Shealtiel: shee-AL-tee-uhl

Shean: SHEE-uhn

Shear: SHEE-uhr

Sheariah: SHEE-uh-**RYE**-uh

Shear Jashub: SHEE-uhr-**JAY**-shuhb

Shear-jashub: SHEE-uhr-**JAY**-shuhb

Shearjashub: SHEE-uhr-**JAY**-shuhb

Sheba: SHEE-buh

Shebah: SHEE-buh

Shebam: SHEE-bam

Shebaniah: SHEB-uh-**NYE**-uh

Shebarim: SHEB-uh-rim

Shebat: SHEE-bat

Sheber: SHEE-buhr

Shebna: SHEB-nuh

Shebnah: SHEB-nuh

Shebuel: sheh-BEW-uhl

Shecaniah: SHEK-uh-**NYE**-uh

Shechaniah: SHEK-uh-**NYE**-uh

Shechem: SHEK-uhm

Shechemite: SHEK-uh-mite

Shedeur: SHED-ee-uhr

Sheerah: SHEE-uh-ruh

Shehariah: SHEE-huh-**RYE**-uh

shekel: SHEK-uhl

Shelah: SHEE-luh

Shelahite: SHEE-luh-hite

Shelanite: SHEE-luh-nite

Shelemiah: SHEL-uh-**MYE**-uh

Sheleph: SHEE-lef

Shelesh: SHEE-lesh

Shelomi: sheh-LOH-mye

Shelomith: sheh-LOH-mith

Shelomoth: sheh-LOH-mahth

Shelumiel: sheh-LOO-mee-uhl

Shem: shem

Shema: SHEE-muh

Shemaah: sheh-MAY-uh

Shemaiah: sheh-MAY-uh

Shemariah: SHEM-uh-**RYE**-uh

Shemeber: shem-EE-buhr

Shemed: SHEE-med

Shemei: SHEM-ee-eye

Shemer: SHEE-muhr

Shemesh: SHEM-esh

Shemiah: sheh-MYE-uh

Shemida: sheh-MYE-duh

Shemidah: sheh-MYE-duh

Shemidaite: sheh-MYE-day-ite

Sheminith: SHEM-uh-nith

Shemiramoth: sheh-MEER-uh-mahth

Shemite: SHEM-ite

Shemoth: SHEE-mahth

Shemuel: SHEM-yoo-uhl

Shen: shen

Shenazar: sheh-NAZ-uhr

Shenazzar: sheh-NAZ-uhr

Shene: SHEE-neh

Shenir: SHEE-nuhr

Sheol: SHEE-ohl

Shepham: SHEE-fuhm

Shephathiah: SHEF-uh-**THYE**-uh

Shephatiah: SHEF-uh-**TYE**-uh

Shephelah: sheh-FEE-luh

Shepher: SHEE-fuhr

Shephi: SHEE-fye

Shepho: SHEE-foh

Shephupham: sheh-FEW-fuhm

Shephuphan: sheh-FEW-fuhn

Sherah: SHEE-ruh

Sherebiah: SHER-uh-**BYE**-uh

Sheresh: SHEER-esh

Sherezer: shuh-REE-zuhr

Sheshach: SHEE-shak

Sheshai: SHEE-shye

Sheshak: SHEE-shak

Sheshan: SHEE-shan

Sheshbazzar: shesh-BAZ-uhr

Sheth: sheth

Shethar: SHEE-thahr

Shethar-baznai: SHEE-thahr-**BAHZ**-nye

Shethar-bozenai: SHEE-thahr-**BAHZ**-uh-nye

Shetharbozenai: SHEE-thahr-**BAHZ**-uh-nye

Shethar-boznai: SHEE-thahr-**BAHZ**-nye

Sheva: SHEE-vuh

Shibah: SHYE-buh

shibboleth: SHIB-uh-leth

Shibmah: SHIB-muh

Shicron: SHIK-rahn

Shiggaion: shuh-GAY-ahn

Shiggionoth: SHIG-ee-**OH**-nahth

Shigionoth: SHIG-ee-**OH**-nahth

Shihon: SHYE-hahn

Shihor: SHY-hor

Shihor Libnath: SHYE-hor-**LIB**-nath

Shihor-libnath: SHYE-hor-**LIB**-nath

Shihorlibnath: SHYE-hor-**LIB**-nath

Shikkeron: SHIK-uh-rahn

Shilhi: SHIL-hye

Shilhim: SHIL-him

Shillem: SHIL-uhm

Shillemite: SHIL-uh-mite

Shiloah: sheh-LOH-uh

Shiloh: SHYE-loh

Shiloni: sheh-LOH-nye

Shilonite: SHYE-luh-nite

Shilshah: SHIL-shuh

Shimea: SHIM-ee-yuh

Shimeah: SHIM-ee-uh

Shimeam: SHIM-ee-uhm

Shimeath: SHIM-ee-ath

Shimeathite: SHIM-ee-uh-thite

Shimei: SHIM-ee-eye

Shimeite: SHIM-ee-ite

Shimeon: SHIM-ee-uhn

Shimhi: SHIM-hye

Shimi: SHIM-eye

Shimite: SHIM-ite

Shimma: SHIM-uh

Shimon: SHY-muhn

Shimrath: SHIM-rath

Shimri: SHIM-rye

Shimrith: SHIM-rith

Shimrom: SHIM-rahm

Shimron: SHIM-rahn

Shimronite: SHIM-ruh-nite

Shimron Meron: SHIM-rahn-**MEE**-rahn

Shimron-meron: SHIM-rahn-**MEE**-rahn

Shimronmeron: SHIM-rahn-**MEE**-rahn

Shimshai: SHIM-shye

shin: shin

Shinab: SHYE-nab

Shinar: SHYE-nahr

Shion: SHYE-uhn

Shiphi: SHYE-fye

Shiphmite: SHIF-mite

Shiphrah: SHIF-ruh

Shiphtan: SHIF-tan

Shir Hashirim: SHEER-**HAH**-shuh-rim

Shisha: SHYE-shuh

Shishak: SHYE-shak

Shitrai: SHIT-rye

Shittah: SHIT-uh

shittah: SHIT-uh

Shittim: SHIT-im

shittim: SHIT-im

Shiza: SHY-zuh

Shoa: SHOH-uh

Shobab: SHOH-bab

Shobach: SHAH-bak

Shobai: SHOH-bye

Shobal: SHOH-buhl

Shobek: SHOH-bek

Shobi: SHOH-bye

Shocho: SHOH-koh

Shochoh: SHOH-koh

Shoco: SHOH-koh

Shofetim: SHOH-fuh-tim

Shoham: SHOH-ham

Shomer: SHOH-muhr

Shophach: SHOH-fak

Shophan: SHOH-fan

Shoshanim: shoh-SHAN-im

Shoshannim: shoh-SHAN-im

Shoshannim Eduth: shoh-SHAN-im-**EE**-duhth

Shoshannim-eduth: shoh-SHAN-im-**EE**-duhth

Shua: SHOO-uh

Shuah: SHOO-uh

Shual: SHOO-uhl

Shubael: SHOO-bay-uhl

Shuh: shoo

Shuhah: SHOO-huh

Shuham: SHOO-ham

Shuhamite: SHOO-huh-mite

Shuhite: SHOO-hite

Shulamite: SHOO-luh-mite

Shulammite: SHOO-luh-mite

Shumathite: SHOO-muh-thite

Shunam: SHOO-nuhm

Shunamite: SHOO-nuh-mite

Shunammite: SHOO-nuh-mite

Shunem: SHOO-nuhm

Shuni: SHOO-nye

Shunite: SHOO-nite

Shupham: SHOO-fuhm

Shuphamite: SHOO-fuh-mite

Shuppim: SHUH-pim

Shuppite: SHUH-pite

Shur: shoor

Shushan: SHOO-shan

Shushanchite: SHOO-shan-kite

Shushan Eduth: SHOO-shan-**EE**-duhth

Shushan-eduth: SHOO-shan-**EE**-duhth

Shuthalhite: SHOO-thuhl-hite

Shuthelah: SHOO-thuh-luh

Shuthelahite: SHOO-thuh-luh-hite

Shuthelaite: SHOO-thuh-lay-ite

Shuthite: SHOO-thite

Sia: SYE-uh

Siaha: SYE-uh-huh

Siba: SYE-buh

Sibbecai: SIB-uh-kye

Sibbechai: SIB-uh-kye

Sibboleth: SIB-uh-leth

Sibmah: SIB-muh

Sibraim: SIB-ray-im

Siceleg: SIK-leg

Sichem: SIK-uhm

sicle: SHEK-uhl

sickle: SHEK-uhl

Sicyon: SISH-ee-uhn

Siddim: SID-im

Side: SYE-dee

Sidon: SYE-duhn

Sidonian: sye-DOH-nee-uhn

Sidrach: SID-rak

Sihon: SYE-hahn

Sihor: SYE-hor

Sikkuth: SIK-uhth

Silas: SYE-luhs

Silla: SIL-uh

Silo: SYE-loh

Siloah: sye-LOH-uh

Siloam: sye-LOH-uhm

Siloni: SYE-loh-nye

Silvanus: sil-VAY-nuhs

Simalcue: seh-MAL-kew-ee

Simeon: SIM-ee-uhn

Simeonite: SIM-ee-uh-nite

Simeron: SIM-uh-rahn

Simmaa: seh-MAY-uh

Simmagir: SIM-uh-guhr

Simon: SYE-muhn

Simon Peter: SYE-muhn-**PEE**-tuhr

Simon-peter: SYE-muhn-**PEE**-tuhr

Simri: SIM-rye

sin: sin

Sina: SYE-nuh

Sinai: SYE-nye

Sinim: SYE-nim

Sinite: SYE-nite

Sion: SYE-uhn

Sior: SYE-or

Siph: sif

Siphmoth: SIF-mahth

Sippai: SIP-eye

Sira: SYE-ruh

Sirach: SYE-ruhk

Sirah: SYE-ruh

Sirion: SEER-ee-uhn

Sisa: SIS-suh

Sisai: SIS-eye

Sisamai: SIS-uh-mye

Sisamoi: SIS-uh-moi

Sisara: SIS-uh-ruh

Sisera: SIS-uh-ruh

Sisinnes: si-SIN-es

Sismai: SIS-mye

sistrum: SIS-troom

Sithri: SITH-rye

Sitnah: SIT-nuh

Siva: SYE-vuh

Sivan: SYE-van

Siyon: SYE-uhn

Siza: SYE-zuh

Smyrna: SMUHR-nuh

So: soh

Soba: Zoba

Sobab: SOH-bab

Sobad: SOH-bad

Sobbochai: SOH-buh-kye

Sobi: SOH-bye

Sobna: SOHB-nuh

Soboba: soh-BOH-buh

Sobochai: SOH-buh-kye

Soccoth: SUHK-uth

Socho: SOH-koh

Sochoh: SOH-koh

Sochothbenoth: SOH-koh-**BEE**-nahth

Soco: SOH-koh

Socoh: SOH-koh

Socoth: SUHK-uth

Sodi: SOH-dye

Sodom: SAHD-uhm

Sodoma: SAHD-uh-muh

Sodomite: SAHD-uh-mite

Sohar: SOH-hahr

Soharite: SOH-huh-rite

Sohoria: SOH-hoh-**RYE**-uh

Solomon: SAHL-uh-muhn

Somer: SOH-muhr

Sopater: SOH-puh-tuhr

Sophach: SOH-fak

Sophai: SOH-fye

Sophan: SOH-fan

Sophar: SOH-fahr

Sopher: SOH-fer

Sophereth: SAHF-uh-rith

Sopherim: SAHF-uh-rim

Sophonias: SOF-uh-**NYE**-uhs

Sorec: SOR-ek

Sorek: SOR-ek

Sores: SOH-rees

Sosipater: soh-**SIP**-uh-tuhr

Sosthenes: SAHS-thuh-neez

Sostratus: SAHS-truh-tuhs

Sotai: SOH-tye

Spain: spayn

Sparta: SPAHR-tuh

Spartan: SPAHR-tuhn

Spirit: SPEER-it

Stachys: STAY-kis

stacte: STAK-tee

stadia: STAY-dee-uh

stater: STAY-tuhr

Stephanas: STEF-uh-nuhs

Stephen: STEE-vuhn

Sthur: SEE-thuhr

Stibic: STI-bik

Stoic: STOH-ik

Stoick: STOH-ik

storax: STOR-aks

Stygian: STI-jee-uhn

Sua: SOO-uh

Suaa: SOO-uh

Suah: SOO-uh

Sual: SOO-uhl

Suar: SOO-ahr

Suba: SOO-buh

Subai: SOO-bye

Subas: SOO-buhs

Sucathite: SOO-kuh-thite

Succoth: SUHK-uhth

Succoth Benoth: SUHK-uhth-**BEE**-nahth

Succoth-benoth: SUHK-uhth-**BEE**-nahth

Succothbenoth: SUHK-uhth-**BEE**-nahth

Suchah: SOO-kuh

Suchathite: SOO-kuh-thite

Sud: suhd

Sudan: SOO-dan

Sudanese: SOO-duh-neez

Sudias: SOO-dee-uhs

Sue: SOO-uh

Suez: SOO-ez

Suham: SOO-ham

Sukkiim: SUHK-ee-im

Sukkite: SUH-kite

Sukkoth: SUHK-uhth

Sunam: SOO-nam

Sunamitess: SOO-nuh-mite-es

Sunem: SOO-nem

Suni: SOO-nye

Suph: soof

Supha: SOO-fuh

Suphah: SOO-fuh

Supham: SOO-fam

Sur: soor

Suriel: soo-RYE-uhl

Surisaddai: SOO-rah-**SAD**-eye

Susa: SOO-suh

Susah: SOO-suh

Susanchite: SOO-suhn-kite

Susanna: soo-ZAN-uh

Susi: SOO-sye

Susian: SOO-see-uhn

Susim: SOO-sim

Suthala: SOO-thuh-luh

sycamine: SIK-uh-meen

Sychar: SYE-kahr

Sychem: SYE-kuhm

Syelus: suh-EE-luhs

Syene: sye-EE-nee

Symeon: SIM-ee-uhn

synagogue: SIN-uh-gahg

Syntyche: SIN-ti-kee

Syracuse: SEER-uh-kewz

Syria: SEER-ee-uh

Syriac: SEER-ee-ak

Syriack: SEER-ee-ak

Syria-damascus: SEER-ee-uh-duh-**MAS**-kuhs

Syria-maachah: SEER-ee-uh-**MAY**-uh-kuh

Syrian: SEER-ee-uhn

Syrophenecian: SYR-roh-feh-**NISH**-uhn

Syro-phoenician: SYR-roh-feh-**NISH**-uhn

Syrophoenician: SYR-roh-feh-**NISH**-uhn

Syrtis: SUHR-tuhs

T

Taanach: TAY-uh-nak

Taanath Shiloh: TAY-uh-nath-**SHYE**-loh

Taanath-shiloh: TAY-uh-nath-**SHYE**-loh

Taanathshiloh: TAY-uh-nath-**SHYE**-loh

Tabaliah: TAB-uh-**LYE**-uh

Tabbaoth: TAB-ay-ahth

Tabbath: TAB-uhth

Tabbur-haares: TAB-uhr-hay-**AHR**-es

Tabeal: TAB-ee-uhl

Tabeel: TAB-ee-uhl

Tabellius: tuh-BEL-ee-uhs

Taberah: TAB-uh-ruh

Tabernacle: **TAB**-uhr-NAK-uhl

Tabitha: TAB-eh-thuh

Tabor: TAY-buhr

Tabremon: tab-REM-uhn

tabret: TAB-ret

Tabrimmon: tab-RIM-uhn

Tabrimon: tab-RIM-uhn

tache: tak

Tachemon: TAK-eh-muhn

Tachmonite: TAK-muh-nite

Tadmor: TAD-mor

Tahan: TAY-han

Tahanite: TAY-huh-nite

Tahapanes: tuh-HAP-uh-neez

Tahash: TAY-hash

Tahath: TAY-hath

Tahchemonite: tah-KEE-muh-nite

Tahkemonite: tah-KEE-muh-nite

Tahpanhes: TAH-puhn-heez

Tahpannes: TAH-puh-neez

Tahpenes: TAH-puh-neez

Tahrea: TAH-ree-uh

Tahtim Hodshi: TAH-tim-**HOD**-shye

Tahtim-hodshi: TAH-tim-**HOD**-shye

talent: TAL-uhnt

talitha cumi: TAL-uh-thuh-**KOO**-mye

talitha-cumi: TAL-uh-thuh-**KOO**-mye

talitha-koum: TAL-uh-thuh-**KOOM**

Talmai: TAL-mye

Talmon: TAL-muhn

Talsas: TAL-suhs

Tamah: TAY-muh

Tamar: TAY-mahr

tamaric: TAM-uh-rik

tamarisk: TAM-uh-risk

Tammuz: TAM-uhz

Tanach: TAY-nak

Tanak: TAY-nak

Tanakh: TAY-nak

Tanhumeth: tan-HEW-meth

Tanis: TAN-is

Taphath: TAY-fath

Tapheth: TAY-fath

Taphnes: TAF-neez

Taphnez: TAF-neez

Taphnis: TAF-neez

Taphon: TAY-fahn

Taphsar: TAF-sahr

Taphua: TAP-yoo-uh

Tappuah: TAP-yoo-uh

Tarah: TAIR-uh

Taralah: TAIR-uh-luh

Tarea: TAIR-ee-uh

Tarpelite: TAHR-puh-lite

Tarshish: TAHR-shish

Tarshishah: TAHR-shuh-shah

Tarsus: TAHR-suhs

Tartak: TAHR-tak

Tartan: TAHR-tan

Tartarus: TAHR-tuh-ruhs

Taschith: TAS-kith

Tatam: TAY-tuhm

Tatnai: TAT-nye

Tattenai: TAT-uh-nye

tau: tou

taw: taw

Tebah: TEE-buh

Tebaliah: TEB-uh-**LYE**-uh

Tebbath: TEE-beth

Tebeth: TEE-beth

Tehaphnehes: tuh-HAF-nuh-heez

Tehillim: tuh-HIL-im

Tehinna: teh-HIN-uh

Tehinnah: teh-HIN-uh

teil: teel

tekel: TEK-uhl

Tekoa: tuh-KOH-uh

Tekoah: tuh-KOH-uh

Tekoite: tuh-KOH-ite

Tel: tel

Tel Abib: TEL-uh-**BEEB**

Tel-abib: TEL-uh-**BEEB**

Telabib: TEL-uh-**BEEB**

Telah: TEE-luh

Telaim: tuh-LAY-im

Telam: TEE-luhm

Tel Assar: tel-AS-ahr

Tel-assar: tel-AS-ahr

Telassar: tel-AS-ahr

Tel Aviv: TEL-uh-**VEEV**

Tel Basar: tel-BAS-ahr

Telem: TEE-lem

Tel-haresha: TEL-huh-**REE**-shuh

Tel-harsa: tel-HAHR-suh

Tel Harsha: tel-HAHR-shuh

Tel-harsha: tel-HAHR-shuh

Telharsha: tel-HAHR-shuh

Tel Melah: tel-MEE-luh

Tel-melah: tel-MEE-luh

Telmelah: tel-MEE-luh

Telmon: TEL-mahn

Tema: TEE-muh

Temah: TEE-muh

Teman: TEE-muhn

Temani: TEE-muh-nye

Temanite: TEE-muh-nite

Temeni: TEM-uh-nye

Temenite: TEM-uh-nite

tenon: TEN-uhn

Tephon: TEE-fahn

Terah: TAIR-uh

teraphim: TAIR-uh-fim

terebinth: TAIR-uh-binth

Teresh: TEER-esh

Tertius: TUHR-shee-uhs

Tertullus: tuhr-TUHL-uhs

Testament: TES-tuh-muhnt

Teta: TAY-tuh

teth: teth

tetrarch: TET-rahrk

Tetter: TET-uhr

Thaan: THAY-an

Thabor: TAY-bohr

Thacasin: thuh-KAY-sin

Thaddaeus: THAD-ee-uhs

Thaddeus: THAD-ee-uhs

Thahash: TAY-hash

Thahath: TAY-hath

Thalassar: thuh-LAS-ahr

Thale: THAY-luh

Thamah: TAY-muh

Thamar: TAY-mahr

Thammuz: TAM-uhz

Thamna: TIM-nah

Thamnata: THAM-nuh-tuh

Thamnatha: THAM-nuh-thuh

Thamnath Saraa: THAM-nath-suh-**RAY**-uh

Thamnathsare: THAM-nath-**SAIR**-uh

Thanac: TAY-nak

Thanach: TAY-nak

Thanath-selo: THAY-nath-**SEE**-loh

Thanehumeth: tan-HEW-meth

Thaphsa: TAF-suh

Thaphua: tap-HEW-uh

Thapsa: TAP-suh

Thara: THAIR-uh

Tharaa: thuh-RAY-uh

Tharaca: thuh-RAY-kuh

Tharana: thuh-RAY-nuh

Thare: THAIR-uh

Tharela: TAIHR-eh-luh

Thares: THAIR-es

Tharra: THAIR-uh

Tharseas: TAHR-see-us

Tharshish: TAHR-shish

Tharsis: TAHR-sis

Tharsus: TAHR-suhs

Tharthac: TAHR-tak

Tharthan: TAHR-tuhn

Thasi: THAS-eye

Thassi: THAS-eye

thau: tou

Thebath: TIB-hath

Thebes: theebz

Thebez: THEE-bez

Thebni: TIB-nye

thecel: TEHK-uhl

Thecoe: thuh-KOH-uh

Thecua: teh-KOO-uh

Thecuite: teh-KOO-ite

Theglathphalasar: TEG-lath-fuh-**LAY**-zuhr

Thehen: TAY-hen

Thelasar: THEL-uh-sahr

Thelassar: THEL-uh-sahr

Thelersas: thuh-LUHR-suhs

Thema: THEE-muh

Theman: THEE-muhn

Themani: THEE-muh-nye

Themna: TIM-nuh

Thenac: TAY-nak

Theocanus: thee-AHK-uh-nuhs

Theodotius: thee-AHD-uh-**TYE**-uhs

Theodotus: thee-AHD-uh-tuhs

Theophilus: thee-AHF-uh-luhs

Theraphim: TAIR-uh-fim

Theras: THEE-ruhs

Thermeleth: thuhr-MEE-lith

Thersa: TUHR-suh

Thesbite: TES-byte

Thessalonian: THES-uh-**LOH**-nee-uhn

Thessalonica: THES-uh-luh-**NYE**-kuh

Theudas: THOO-duhs

Thilon: TY-luhn

Thimnathah: TIM-nuh-thuh

Thiras: TYE-ruhs

Thiria: TEER-ee-uh

Thisbe: THIS-bee

Thochen: TOH-ken

Thogorma: toh-GAHR-muh

Thohu: TOH-hew

Thola: TOH-luh

Tholad: TOH-lad

Tholaite: TOH-lay-ite

Tholmai: TAHL-mye

Thomas: TOM-uhs

Thomoi: THAHM-oi

Thophel: TOH-fel

Thopo: TOH-poh

Thosaite: TOH-say-ite

Thou: TOH-uh

Thracian: THRAY-shee-uhn

Thraseas: thray-SEE-uhs

Thraseos: thray-SEE-uhs

Thubal: TOO-buhl

Thummim: THUHM-im

Thyatira: THYE-uh-**TYE**-ruh

thyine: THYE-in

Tiberias: tye-BEER-ee-uhs

Tiberius: tye-BEER-ee-uhs

Tibhath: TIB-hath

Tibni: TIB-nye

Tichon: TYE-kuhn

Ticon: TYE-kuhn

Tidal: TYE-duhl

Tiglath-pileser: TIG-lath-pye-**LEE**-zuhr

Tiglathpileser: TIG-lath-pye-**LEE**-zuhr

Tigris: TYE-gris

Tikvah: TIK-vuh

Tikvath: TIK-vath

Tilgath-pilneser: TIL-gath-pil-**NEE**-zuhr

Tilgathpilneser: TIL-gath-pil-**NEE**-zuhr

Tilon: TYE-luhn

Timaeus: tye-MEE-uhs

Timna: TIM-nuh

Timnah: TIM-nuh

Timnah-serah: TIM-nuh-**SEER**-uh

Timnath: TIM-nath

Timnath Heres: TIM-nath-**HEE**-rez

Timnath-heres: TIM-nath-**HEE**-rez

Timnathheres: TIM-nath-**HEE**-rez

Timnath Serah: TIM-nath-**SEER**-uh

Timnath-serah: TIM-nath-**SEER**-uh

Timnathserah: TIM-nath-**SEER**-uh

Timnite: TIM-nite

Timon: TYE-muhn

Timotheus: ti-MOH-thee-us

Timothy: TIM-oh-thee

Tiphsah: TIF-suh

Tira: TYE-ruh

Tiras: TYE-ruhs

Tirathite: TYE-ruh-thite

Tirhakah: tuhr-HAY-kuh

Tirhanah: tuhr-HAY-nuh

Tiria: TEER-ee-uh

Tirshatha: tuhr-SHAY-thuh

Tirzah: TEER-zuh

Tishbe: TISH-bee

Tishbite: TISH-bite

Titan: TYE-tuhn

Titius: TISH-ee-uhs

Titius Justus: TISH-ee-uhs-**JUHS**-tuhs

tittle: TIT-uhl

Titus: TYE-tuhs

Tiz: tiz

Tizite: TIZ-ite

Toah: TOH-uh

Tob: tahb

Tob-adonijah: TAHB-ad-uh-**NYE**-juh

Tobadonijah: TAHB-ad-uh-**NYE**-juh

Tobiad: toh-BYE-uhd

Tobiah: toh-BYE-uh

Tobias: toh-BYE-uhs

Tobie: TOH-bee

Tobiel: TOH-bee-uhl

Tobijah: toh-BYE-juh

Tobit: TOH-bit

Tochen: TOH-kuhn

Togarmah: toh-GAHR-muh

Tohu: TOH-hew

Toi: toi

Token: TOH-ken

Tokhath: TOK-hath

Tola: TOH-luh

Tolad: TOH-lad

Tolaite: TOH-lay-ite

Tolbanes: TAHL-buh-neez

Tolmai: TAHL-mye

Tophel: TOH-fuhl

Tophet: TOH-fit

Topheth: TOH-fith

Torah: TOH-ruh

Tormah: TOR-muh

Tou: too

Toubiani: TOO-bee-**AY**-nee

Trachonitis: TRAK-uh-**NYE**-tis

Traconitis: TRAK-uh-**NYE**-tis

Trans-euphrates: TRANS-yoo-**FRAY**-teez

Transeuphrates: TRANS-yoo-**FRAY**-teez

Trans-jordan: trans-JOR-duhn

Transjordan: trans-JOR-duhn

tribunal: trye-BEW-nuhl

tribune: TRIB-yoon

trigon: TRYE-gahn

Tripolis: TRIP-uh-lis

Troas: TROH-az

Trogyllium: troh-JIL-ee-uhm

Trophimus: TRAHF-uh-muhs

Tryphaena: trye-FEE-nuh

Tryphena: trye-FEE-nuh

Trypho: TRYE-foh

Tryphon: TRYE-fuhn

Tryphosa: trye-FOH-suh

Tubal: TOO-buhl

Tubal-cain: **TOO**-buhl-KAYN

Tubalcain: **TOO**-buhl-KAYN

Tubian: TOO-bee-uhn

Tubianite: TOO-bee-uhn-ite

Tubieni: TOO-bee-**EE**-nee

Tubin: TOO-bin

Tychicus: TIK-uh-kuhs

Tyrannus: teh-RAN-uhs

Tyre: tyer

Tyrian: TEER-ee-uhn

Tyrus: TYE-ruhs

tzaddi: TSAHD-ee

U

Ucal: YOO-kuhl

Uel: YOO-uhl

Uknaz: UHK-naz

Ulai: YOO-lye

Ulam: YOO-luhm

Ulla: UHL-uh

Ummah: UHM-uh

unction: UHNK-shuhn

Unni: UHN-eye

Unno: UHN-oh

upharsin: yoo-FAHR-sin

Uphaz: YOO-faz

Ur: uhr

Urai: YOOR-eye

Urbane: UHR-bayn

Urbanus: uhr-BAY-nuhs

Uri: YOOR-eye

Uriah: yoo-RYE-uh

Urias: yoo-RYE-uhs

Uriel: YOOR-ee-uhl

Urijah: yoo-RYE-juh

Urim: YOOR-im

Urukian: yoo-ROOK-ee-uhn

Usal: YOO-zuhl

Uthai: YOO-thye

Uz: uhz

Uzai: YOO-zye

Uzal: YOO-zuhl

Uzza: UHZ-uh

Uzzah: UHZ-uh

Uzzen Sheerah: UHZ-uhn-**SHEE**-uh-ruh

Uzzen-sheerah: UHZ-uhn-**SHEE**-uh-ruh

Uzzensheerah: UHZ-uhn-**SHEE**-uh-ruh

Uzzen Sherah: UHZ-uhn-**SHEE**-ruh

Uzzen-sherah: UHZ-uhn-**SHEE**-ruh

Uzzi: UHZ-eye

Uzzia: uh-ZYE-uh

Uzziah: uh-ZYE-uh

Uzziel: UHZ-ee-uhl

Uzzielite: UHZ-ee-uh-lite

V

Vaheb: VAY-heb

Vaizatha: VYE-zuh-thuh

Vajezatha: vuh-JEZ-uh-thuh

Vale-Casis: VAY-luh-**KAY**-sis

Vaniah: vuh-NYE-uh

Vapsi: VAP-sye

Vashni: VASH-nye

Vashti: VASH-tye

Vasseni: vah-SEN-nye

vau: vou

Vedan: VEE-duhn

victuals: VIT-uhls

Vophsi: VAHF-sye

W

Wadi: WAH-dee

Waheb: WAY-heb

waw: wou

Weeks: weeks

wen: wen

Wisdom: WIZ-duhm

X

Xanthicus: ZAN-thi-kuhs

Xerxes: ZUHRK-seez

Y

Yad-abshalom: yahd-AB-shuh-luhm

Yah: yah

Yahweh: YAH-weh

Yahweh-nissi: YAH-weh-**NIS**-eye

Yahweh-shalom: YAH-weh-shah-**LOHM**

Yahweh-yireh: YAH-weh-**YEER**-eh

Yaudi: YAW-dye

Yavan: YAY-vuhn

Yehezqel: yuh-HEZ-kuhl

Yehoshua: yuh-HOSH-yoo-uh

Yeshayahu: YEH-shah-**YAH**-hoo

Yirmeyahu: YEER-muh-**YAH**-hoo

Yiron: YEER-uhn

yodh: yohd

Z

Zaanaim: ZAY-uh-**NAY**-im

Zaanan: ZAY-uh-nan

Zaanannim: ZAY-uh-**NA**-nim

Zaavan: ZAY-uh-vuhn

Zabad: ZAY-bad

Zabadaius: ZAB-uh-**DAY**-yuhs

Zabadean: ZAB-uh-**DEE**-uhn

Zabadia: ZAB-uh-**DYE**-uh

Zabdi: ZAB-dye

Zabdiel: ZAB-dee-uhl

Zabud: ZAY-buhd

Zabulon: ZAB-yuh-luhn

Zaccai: ZAK-eye

Zacchaeus: za-KEE-uhs

Zaccheus: za-KEE-uhs

Zacchur: ZAK-uhr

Zaccur: ZAK-uhr

Zachai: ZAK-eye

Zachariah: ZAK-uh-**RYE**-uh

Zacharias: ZAK-uh-**RYE**-uhs

Zacher: ZAY-kuhr

Zachur: ZAY-kuhr

Zadok: ZAY-dahk

Zadokite: ZAY-duh-kite

Zaham: ZAY-ham

Zahar: ZAY-hahr

zain: ZAH-yin

Zair: ZAY-uhr

Zakkur: ZAK-uhr

Zalaph: ZAY-lif

Zalmon: ZAL-muhn

Zalmonah: zal-MOH-nuh

Zalmunna: zal-MUHN-uh

Zambri: ZAM-brye

Zamira: zuh-MYE-ruh

Zamma: ZAM-uh

Zamoth: ZAY-mahth

Zamran: ZAM-ran

Zamri: ZIM-rye

Zamzummim: zam-ZUH-mim

Zamzummin: zam-ZUH-min

Zamzummite: zam-ZUH-mite

Zannanim: zuh-NAY-nim

Zanoah: zuh-NOH-uh

Zanoe: zuh-NOH-uh

Zaphaniah: ZAF-uh-**NYE**-uh

Zaphenath-paneah: ZAF-uh-nath-puh-**NEE**-uh

Zaphenathpaneah: ZAF-uh-nath-puh-**NEE**-uh

Zaphnath-paaneah: ZAF-nath-pay-uh-**NEE**-uh

Zaphon: ZAY-fahn

Zara: ZAIR-uh

Zaraces: ZAIR-uh-seez

Zarah: ZAIR-uh

Zarahia: ZAIR-uh-**HIGH**-uh

Zaraias: zuh-RAY-uhs

Zare: ZAIR-uh

Zareah: ZAIR-ee-uh

Zareathite: ZAIR-ee-uh-thite

Zared: ZAY-red

Zarephath: ZAIR-uh-fath

Zaretan: ZAIR-uh-tan

Zareth-shahar: ZAIR-eth-**SHAY**-hahr

Zarethan: ZAIR-uh-than

Zarhite: ZAHR-hite

Zarius: ZAIR-ee-uhs

Zartanah: ZAHR-tuh-nuh

Zarthan: ZAHR-than

Zathoe: ZATH-oh-ee

Zathui: ZATH-oo-ee

Zatthu: ZAT-thoo

Zattu: ZAT-oo

Zavan: ZAY-vuhn

zayin: ZAH-yin

Zaza: ZAY-zuh

Zealot: ZEL-uht

Zeb: zeb

Zebadiah: ZEB-uh-**DYE**-uh

Zebah: ZEE-buh

Zebaim: zuh-BAY-im

Zebedee: ZEB-uh-dee

Zebee: ZEB-ee-uh

Zebida: zuh-BYE-duh

Zebidah: zuh-BYE-duh

Zebina: zuh-BYE-nuh

Zeboiim: zuh-BOI-im

Zeboim: zuh-BOH-im

Zebub: ZEE-buhb

Zebudah: zuh-BEW-duh

Zebul: ZEE-buhl

Zebulonite: ZEB-yuh-luh-nite

Zebulun: ZEB-yuh-luhn

Zebulunite: ZEB-yuh-luh-nite

Zechariah: ZEK-uh-**RYE**-uh

Zecher: ZEE-kuhr

Zechri: ZEK-rye

Zechur: ZEK-oor

Zedad: ZEE-dad

Zedechias: ZED-uh-**KYE**-uhs

Zedekiah: ZED-uh-**KYE**-uh

Zeeb: ZEE-uhb

Zeker: ZEE-kuhr

Zela: ZEE-luh

Zelah: ZEE-luh

Zelek: ZEE-lek

Zelophehad: zuh-LOH-fuh-had

Zelotes: zuh-LOH-teez

Zelzah: ZEL-zuh

Zemaraim: ZEM-uh-**RAY**-im

Zemarite: ZEM-uh-rite

Zemer: ZEE-muhr

Zemira: zuh-MYE-ruh

Zemirah: zuh-MYE-ruh

Zenan: ZEE-nuhn

Zenas: ZEE-nuhs

Zephaniah: ZEF-uh-**NYE**-uh

Zephath: ZEE-fath

Zephathah: ZEF-uh-thuh

Zephi: ZEE-fye

Zepho: ZEE-foh

Zephon: ZEE-fahn

Zephonite: ZEE-fuh-nite

Zephrona: ZEF-roh-nuh

Zer: zuhr

Zerah: ZEER-uh

Zerahiah: ZER-uh-**HYE**-uh

Zerahite: ZEER-uh-hite

Zeraiah: zuh-RAY-uh

Zerdaiah: zer-DAY-uh

Zered: ZEER-ed

Zereda: ZER-uh-duh

Zeredah: ZER-uh-duh

Zeredatha: ZER-uh-**DAY**-thuh

Zererah: ZER-uh-ruh

Zererath: ZER-uh-rath

Zeresh: ZEER-esh

Zereth: ZEER-eth

Zereth Shahar: ZEER-eth-**SHAY**-hahr

Zereth-shahar: ZEER-eth-**SHAY**-hahr

Zerethshahar: ZEER-eth-**SHAY**-hahr

Zeri: ZEER-eye

Zeror: ZEER-or

Zeruah: zuh-ROO-uh

Zerubbabel: zuh-RUHB-uh-buhl

Zeruiah: zuh-ROO-yuh

Zetham: ZEE-thuhm

Zethan: ZEE-thuhn

Zethar: ZEE-thahr

Zeus: zoos

Zia: ZYE-uh

Ziba: ZYE-buh

Zibeon: ZIB-ee-uhn

Zibia: ZIB-ee-uh

Zibiah: ZIB-ee-uh

Zichri: ZIK-rye

Zicri: ZIK-rye

Ziddim: ZID-im

Zidkijah: zid-KYE-juh

Zidon: ZYE-duhn

Zidonian: zye-DOH-nee-uhn

Zie: ZYE-uh

Zif: zif

Ziha: ZYE-huh

Ziklag: ZIK-lag

Zikri: ZIK-rye

Zillah: ZIL-uh

Zillethai: ZIL-uh-thye

Zilpah: ZIL-puh

Zilthai: ZIL-thye

Zimmah: ZIM-uh

Zimran: ZIM-ran

Zimri: ZIM-rye

Zin: zin

Zina: ZYE-nuh

Zio: ZYE-oh

Zion: ZYE-uhn

Zior: ZYE-or

Ziph: zif

Zipha: ZYE-fuh

Ziphah: ZYE-fuh

Ziphim: ZIF-im

Ziphion: ZIF-ee-uhn

Ziphite: ZIF-ite

Ziphron: ZIF-rahn

Zippor: ZIP-or

Zipporah: zi-POR-uh

Zithri: ZITH-rye

Ziv: ziv

Ziz: ziz

Ziza: ZYE-zuh

Zizah: ZYE-zuh

Zoan: ZOH-uhn

Zoar: ZOH-ahr

Zoba: ZOH-buh

Zobab: ZOH-bab

Zobach: ZOH-bak

Zobad: ZOH-bad

Zobah: ZOH-buh

Zobal: ZOH-bal

Zobebah: zoh-BEE-buh

Zodiac: ZOH-dee-ak

Zohar: ZOH-hahr

Zoheleth: ZOH-huh-leth

Zoheth: ZOH-heth

Zomzommim: zahm-ZAHM-im

Zoof: zuhf

Zophah: ZOH-fuh

Zophai: ZOH-fye

Zophar: ZOH-fahr

Zophim: ZOH-fim

Zorah: ZOR-uh

Zorathite: ZOR-uh-thite

Zoreah: zoh-REE-uh

Zores: ZOH-reez

Zorite: ZOR-ite

Zorobabel: zoh-RAHB-uh-buhl

Zuar: ZOO-uhr

Zuph: zuhf

Zuphite: ZOO-fite

Zur: zuhr

Zuriel: ZOOR-ee-uhl

Zurishaddai: ZOOR-i-**SHAD**-eye

Zuth: zooth

Zuzim: ZOO-zim

Zuzite: ZOO-zite

Companion Product

As of the time of the writing of this book, an app is being written to enable users to hear each name being pronounced. If you would like to purchase this app when it becomes available, please go to EasyBibleNamesApp.com/guide to add your name to our mailing list. We'll let you know via email just as soon as it is available.

About the Author

Steven K. Webb is a husband, a father and a grandfather who yielded to the call of God's love at the age of sixteen years.

He readily admits to his frequent need of the cleansing power of the infinite, unfathomable grace that the sacrifice of Jesus makes available to anyone who has a personal relationship with Him.

In 2004 God led Steve to start the world's first Christian podcast not based on repurposed church sermons. (LifespringMedia.com) An outgrowth of that podcast was another, on which Steve read the Bible through in a year. It was while recording the daily installments of this podcast that he began to feel the need for an easy-to-use Bible names pronunciation guide.

In 2008 Steve became a professional voice-over artist. Less than a year after making this transition, he was commissioned to record the Douay-Rheims Audio Bible. (DouayRheimsAudioBible.com)

Upon finding no resources to help with the pronunciation of the names found in this very old Catholic translation of the Bible (it predates the King James Version), even after consulting with Catholic scholars, he set out to create a pronunciation guide for his own use to aid him in the work of recording the Douay.

Having an extensive library of Christian reference books in his home, and with the added benefit of the internet, Steve carefully researched each name to arrive at the pronunciations printed in this book. The work took two and a half years.

Somewhere during this time, it occurred to Steve that there were probably many other people who could benefit from his research, so he began to include the spellings of Bible names from every English translation he could find, with an eye toward publishing his guide. It is possible that some spellings have been left out of this book, but they will be included in future editions if necessity dictates.

Steve's sincere prayer is that you will find this book to be a help to you as you seek to serve God in whatever way He calls you.

For more information about Steve, please visit LifespringMedia.com/about-steve-webb.

Notes

Made in the USA
Lexington, KY
07 March 2018